Oh read me a story and let me forget

This brain racking worry, this wearying fret

Read me of when the harp was still strung

To the bold and free ditty the minstrel had sung;

When at my lord's coming the joy bells were rung

When all hearts were merry and the world was still young

When honor was common and knavery rare

The men were all gallant, the women all fair:

And when sweetest sad music was heard in the air

Sailors knew that mermaidens were combing their hair.

So come read the tale, dear, and let us forget

This present day hurry and struggle and fret.

—Laura Ingalls Wilder

A Little House Reader

A Collection of Writings by
LAURA INGALLS WILDER

Edited by William Anderson

HarperCollins*Publishers*

Photographs on pages viii, 6, 17, 31, 47, 53, 56, 58, 81, 96, 120, 135, 147, 149, 164, 168, 178, 192, and 194 courtesy of the Laura Ingalls Wilder Home Association, Mansfield, Missouri. Photographs on pages 22, 26, 104, 112, 116, and 189 courtesy of the Herbert Hoover Presidential Library, West Branch, Iowa.
Photograph on page 3 courtesy of the Aubrey Sherwood Collection, De Smet, South Dakota.
Photographs on pages 36, 62, 63, 66, 86, 99, 123, 162, and 190 from the editor's collection.

A Little House Reader
A Collection of Writings by Laura Ingalls Wilder
Text copyright © 1998 by William Anderson

Library of Congress Cataloging-in-Publication Data
Wilder, Laura Ingalls, 1867-1957.
    A Little house reader : a collection of writings / by Laura Ingalls Wilder ; edited by William Anderson.
        p.   cm.
    Summary: a collection of articles, essays, poems, and other writings which shows that the author known for her Little House books was a prolific and talented writer all her life.
    ISBN 0-06-026358-X. — ISBN 0-06-026394-6 (lib. bdg.)
    1. Frontier and pioneer life—United States—Literary collections. 2. Frontier and pioneer life—United States. [1. Wilder, Laura Ingalls, 1867—1957. 2. Authors, American. 3. Frontier and pioneer life.] I. Anderson, William. II. Title.
PS3545.I342A6   1998   97-2767
813'.52—dc21   CIP
                                                                       AC

1   2   3   4   5   6   7   8   9   10   ❖   First Edition

CONTENTS

Laura in 1906, at age thirty-nine.

PROLOGUE

"I was amazed, because I didn't know how to write."

That was the modest response that Laura Ingalls Wilder gave when she was asked to explain the success of the books she wrote in her sixties and seventies, which are known collectively as the Little House books. When the first volume appeared soon after her sixty-fifth birthday in 1932, Laura was hailed as an exciting newcomer to the field of children's books. Few thought to question how the Ozark farm woman had bridged the gap from the henhouse to the publishing house.

In reality, Laura's writing life stretched back more than fifty years. It was born in the same prairie homes she described in the Little House books. Yet nowhere do her written memories of her pioneer childhood speak of evenings bent over the writing tablets in the glow of the flickering kerosene lamp. No scrap of her poetry was incorporated in her books, except for a solitary jingle in *Little Town on the Prairie* she composed to show her dislike for a teacher.

In the first compilation of long-lost or previously unpublished Wilder writings, *A Little House Sampler* (HarperCollins, 1989), I gathered together the written words of both Laura and her daughter, Rose Wilder Lane, to tell the tale of nearly a century of family life lived by these pioneers. When the book was published, letters poured in, asking for more. "When will we see more of Laura's poetry?" one asked.

"What else did Laura write?" asked another. Others said they wished to read the writings of the other members of Laura's family. And often the question was asked whether Laura kept daily diaries.

Unfortunately, Laura did not keep a diary, save on trips she took, such as the one she described in *On the Way Home* (Harper & Row, 1962). But as I dug deeper into the Wilder writings, I was amazed to learn that Laura had composed poems nearly all her life, that she had described the building of her Rocky Ridge farmhouse in detail, and that she had written down her strong political views and well-thought-out theories on the place of farm families in society. Laura's writings, in fact, far from being confined to her older years, spanned a lifetime; from the little cabin in the woods of Wisconsin to her death at the age of ninety, there was seldom a time that Laura was not exploring the world around her through words. Her occasional jottings about God and nature round out the beliefs of a woman who found beauty in simplicity but thought far and wide about matters of time and eternity.

As I read more and more of Laura's writings, it became clear to me that the audience that loved her for her Little House books would welcome the opportunity to get to know her better through her other writings, which range from adolescent poetry to newspaper columns on the role of farmwives to musings on life and death. While I have included some essays and poems by Laura's parents and her sisters, *A Little House Reader* is really Laura's book and is intended to complete the portrait of the woman known best for her final writings, the Little House books.

This collection is culled for the most part from Laura's private writings; the paper she wrote on is now yellowing and brittle. The writings in this collection are arranged to mirror significant periods in her long life. Her early jottings as a pioneer girl demonstrate her smooth writing voice, which later served her well as she described the building of her Rocky Ridge farmhouse and expressed her thoughts as a community leader, a country journalist, a mature poet, a beloved author, and a wise old woman looking at both the past and the future.

Rose Wilder Lane's heir, Roger MacBride, eventually became the guardian of the Wilder family papers. Under his careful direction, books such as *The First Four Years* (Harper & Row, 1971) and *West from Home* (Harper & Row, 1974) made their appearances. Roger's encouragement at the inception of this *Little House Reader* was cut short by his sudden death in March 1995. But his suggestions and enthusiasm and permission to quote from the various manuscripts are all gratefully acknowledged.

Fortunately for history's sake, Laura Ingalls Wilder saved nearly every scrap of paper she ever wrote on. So, as a new century looms, she can still speak to and inspire us as we move ahead to pioneer our own frontiers.

William Anderson
January 1998

A Family of Writers

Tales of lonely cowboys reading Shakespeare around campfires and accounts of pioneers transporting barrels of treasured books along the overland trails are not uncommon in the history of the westward movement. The pioneers often clung to vestiges of their previous culture and education as they faced the uncertain challenges of the frontier.

Fortunately, the pioneers both read and wrote. Their letters and journals chronicle their trials and adventures, and offer a glimpse into what was an exciting and often dangerous life. "People kept journals then," remarked Rose Wilder Lane. "Their lives were so interesting to them, they got all they could out of every minute and then wrote it down to remember." Rose's own family was no exception. Throughout the covered-wagon travels described in the Little House books, the Ingalls family read, wrote, and recorded what Laura once called the "fascination and terror" of pioneering.

When Laura Ingalls Wilder became well known for her writings, she was asked to explain her skill and talent with words. "The only reason I can think of for being able to write at all was that both Father and Mother were great readers and I read a lot at home with them." Laura's response was based on her memories of the many books the Ingallses owned. Despite their limited finances, the Ingalls family owned what amounted in the mid-nineteenth century to a small home library. Works of Dickens, Shakespeare, Pope, Scott, Henry Ward Beecher, and other popular authors of the day fed the family's craving for the printed word. Biographies and travel accounts instructed them about life beyond their frontier setting. They eagerly received newspapers and magazines of the day, including The St. Paul Pioneer Press; The Chicago Inter-Ocean; The Youth's Companion, *which was a magazine specifically for children and young adults; and a church paper,* The Advance. *After settling down in De Smet, they avidly read both weekly local papers,* The De Smet News and Leader *and* The Kingsbury County News.

Laura's family was a reading family; they were also a writing family. Often their own lives provided the Ingalls family with a reason to write. For many years, members of the Quiner and Ingalls clans participated in a circulating letter. Each branch of the family added its own news and sent the letter ahead to the next recipient. These letters continued for two generations, keeping the far-flung pioneering relatives abreast of each other's movements and lives.

❈ Charles Phillip Ingalls ❈

Laura's Pa, Charles Ingalls, was not only a skilled spinner of yarns, an aspect of his personality that Laura immortalized in her books, but he also wrote down periodic accounts of his life. He kept a weather diary, and he jotted down information and helpful farming tips that he valued. In a railroad ledger from his days working as storekeeper for the Chicago and Northwestern Railroad, also known as the Dakota Central Railroad, he used blank pages to record highlights of the early beginnings of De Smet, the Dakota town in which he and his family finally settled, and

De Smet's Calumet Avenue ("Main Street"), as it looked in 1883; this is probably one of the earliest photographs of the town.

about which Laura herself wrote in By the Shores of Silver Lake, The Long Winter, Little Town on the Prairie, *and* These Happy Golden Years. *Grace discovered her father's account in 1930 and excitedly shared the news with her sisters.*

THE SETTLING OF DE SMET

I, Charles P. Ingalls and family arrived at Silver Lake Sep. 9, 1879 and worked for A. L. Wells and Co selling goods to the graders on the Dakota Central Railroad. Worked until Dec. 1st, 1879. Then the graders quit work and left for the east and we moved into the Company's building for the winter.

When I and my family were left alone for the winter on

the prairie without neighbors we used to say we neighbored with Nelson, who lived on the Jim River 37 miles to the West of us.[*] Walter Ogden, a single man that was working for Henry Peck stayed with us taking care of teams belonging to Peck that were left here for the winter.

We used to keep a lamp burning in the window for fear that some one might try to cross the prairie from the Sioux River to the Jim River and that light brought in some to shelter that must otherwise have perished on the prairie. The coyotes used to come to the door and pick up the crumbs that were scattered.

About the last day of December on a bitter cold night, I think it was the coldest night during the winter, some one called out at the door. Upon going to the door what was my surprise to see a woman on horseback but upon looking a second time I saw a man also, it was R. A. Boast and wife that had come to stay and you may be sure we felt as though we had got back to civilization again. They moved into a small house that had been put up for an office by an enterprising man.

About the first of February travel commenced between the Sioux and the Jim Rivers, then we had company in plenty. Some nights there was so many that they covered the floor as thick as they could lay down.

The first of March 1880, I commenced to build a house on the towncite of De Smet. A man by the name of Bierdsly[†] commenced a hotel about the same time. E. M. Harthorn

---

[*] The town of Huron was established on the James River.
[†] The actual spelling was Beardsley.

began the erection of a store a few days after. V. V. Barnes came about the 12th of March 1880 with some lumber for a shanty on his claim ½ mile west of De Smet. He put up his shanty and went to bed in it. He had blankets with him and a thermometer which he hung up by the head of his bed. In the morning when he awoke and looked at the thermometer it was 12 degrees below zero. I well remember seeing him coming across the prairie towards the house and you may be sure he did not come slow.

I forgot to mention that I made a trip to Brookings in February and took a homestead. The N.E. ¾ section 3 town 110 range 56. In April there was a good many settlers come to De Smet and vicinity and they commenced to talk about the organization of the county. The first commissioners appointed were H. J. Burvee of Spirit Lake, Ben Loken of Lake Whitewood. J. H. Carrol was appointed clerk of court, R. S. Fieldby Sheriff, Amos Whiting Superintendent of Schools. During the summer there was 16 buildings put up on the town cite, besides the depot.

❀ Caroline Quiner Ingalls ❀

Laura's mother, too, was a writer. Early in her life, Caroline Quiner Ingalls knew of hardship and tragedy. Her father, Henry Newton Quiner, was lost in the shipwreck of a schooner on Lake Michigan during the fall of 1844 when Caroline was just five years old. A decade later, she wrote "The Ocean," a school composition that reflected both the natural majesty and the potential terror of the water.

Charles and Caroline Ingalls, circa 1880.

THE OCEAN

What a world of beauty there is in the Ocean! Look upon it in a calm, and it fills us with awe and admiration. How it sparkles as the sun shines upon it in all its splendor, and how lovely and majestic the ships look sailing upon its smooth and placid surface. Imagine a ship coming into port, on a calm and pleasant day. A great number of people have congregated to witness the scene, and welcome their friends, who have been spared to return in safety, to them after an absence of perhaps months.

Then imagine a ship on the water in a storm. What a contrast! All is hurry and confusion on board, for every hand must be at work, to save the ship if possible. And how often the ship, and its whole crew, find a grave in the bed of the ocean and become the food of animals of the deep. Who can picture the sufferings of the survivors, on board a wreck? Perhaps no more than three or four remains of a crew of some hundred persons and they must be tossed about at the mercy of the winds and waves, for many days, with hardly food enough to sustain life. Then some passing ship may pick them up when life is almost extinct; or perhaps after all their sufferings and endeavors to get ashore, or attract the attention of some passing ship, they perish. Then think of the homes made desolate by such events.

As a seasoned pioneer woman who moved many times in the course of her life, Caroline also knew the hardships of packing, sorting, and leaving behind treasured possessions as she prepared for moves into unknown territories. Like thousands of other women during the era of westward migration, she bade farewell to friends and family, knowing full well she might never see them again. Her pioneering trek began in 1862, when she left settled farm country near Concord, Wisconsin, and journeyed with her husband and his family into the northern forests of the state near Lake Pepin. From there, she and Charles moved to Kansas and back, to Minnesota and Iowa, and finally to Dakota Territory. In 1879, the Ingalls family finally put down roots near the town of De Smet. Charles Ingalls would have continued to travel west to the Pacific coast, but Caroline's love of home and desire to have their daughters properly educated prevailed. So in De Smet the Ingallses stayed, and they became solid, well-liked citizens of the town. After a married life of constant travel, Caroline gratefully established her household in the final Ingalls home, which Charles built in 1887. She lived there happily until her death in 1924. Among her keepsakes, her daughters found her thoughts on "Home," written before her marriage in 1860.

HOME

How sweet and endearing is the name of home! What music in that sacred sound!

It is there we can have the society of our beloved parents, brothers, and sisters; and how delightful it is after the avocations of the day to assemble around the bright, blazing fire variously employed: perhaps one with a book, to read aloud some interesting story, for the benefit and amusement of us all.

Although the wind is whistling without and blowing the snow, in every direction, making drifts as high as the fences; yet we heed it not. But we oftentimes think of and pity those who have no comfortable home, to secure them from the inclemency of the weather.

Who could wish to leave home and wander forth in the world to meet its tempests and its storms? Without a mother's watchful care and a sister's tender love? Not one.

They would very likely meet with some warm friends, and some that would try to make it pleasant for them, and appear as much like home as possible, for which they would be very grateful. Yet after all it would not be like home.

❁ Mary Amelia Ingalls ❁

Laura was not the only Ingalls girl who wrote. Rather, writings from all three of her sisters have been found among the Ingalls papers. These writings range from diary entries to published poems, and all show a desire to record history and memories in a time long before the telephone and video recorders. Mary Ingalls, in particular, spent a good deal of her adult life composing poetry. When she lost her eyesight in 1879, at the age of fourteen, one of the harshest realities both for Mary herself and for her family was the realization that her own budding talents in writing and her goal of becoming a teacher might never be realized. Only two years later, Mary was enrolled at the Iowa College for the Blind. Under its progressive tutelage, Mary blossomed in music, reading, history, writing, and handwork.

Mary's years at the college were a highlight in what would be a quiet, contented life. She had the opportunity to delve into the studies she had always craved, she received up-to-date training for the sightless, and she was able to mingle with many other students of her own age. A close friend and classmate, Anna Swann, received this poem from Mary.

Pressed Flowers from Memory's Coffer

In a casket of keepsakes hidden away
My dearest treasure lies
A cluster of flowers, a tiny bouquet
Which love will always prize
Symbols of purity are daisies white
Of love, are scarlet flowers
Together they bloomed on that parting night
Brightening the last sad hours.

Together we stood in the gleaming light
Together bade farewell
To friends whom we loved in the old bright days
With grief we could not tell
Oh would that those days which are gone for aye*
Might come but once again
For sake of the pleasures passed away
I'd once more bear the pain
The flowers I wore I pressed in a book

---

* Always, forever.

Sweet memories in my heart
Swiftly tears come to my eyes as I look
And think how soon to part
From the orbit of life our dearest friends'
Fond hopes soon decay
As circle with tangent an instant blends
Then meets no more for aye.

As the delicate blossoms shed their bloom
Ere scarce they had been seen
Or beautiful visions fade into gloom
Sad heart 'twas but a dream,
A dream of love, No! No! it cannot be
The love my heart holds dear
Will glow and burn through all eternity
Its fleeting shadow here
As raindrops falling through the blue
Mingle their waters bright
Then parting each bears in its rainbow hue
Gleams of the other's light
So friends though far from each other they rove
Hold in the inmost heart
The rosy glow of eternal love
And true friends never part.

Mary was twenty-four when she graduated from college in 1889,
and she continued to take an interest in poetry when she returned
to live at home with her family in De Smet. Her poems were

all neatly recopied in her mother's hand, and many of them mark special events or occasions. Several of Mary's poems were published during her lifetime, most probably in the church paper The Advance. *Knowing that her work appeared in print no doubt gave Mary the same quiet satisfaction that seemed to mark the rest of her life with her parents and sisters in the family home in De Smet. "How good it is to be alive!" Mary exclaimed in a letter to Laura in 1914. "So let us be thankful that we were born. Let us fold away our fears and put by our foolish tears through the coming year and just be glad." Mary's poem "A Birthday Meditation" was published: An undated clipping from a newspaper was found among her aunt Martha Carpenter's papers.*

A Birthday Meditation

Another year is ended,
And still my skies are bright,
For hope and faith are blended,
And all will soon be right.
A song of praise is welling
From out my heart today,
Of the thousand blessings telling
That lie along the way.

Thanks be to God for giving
This life to me at all,
Though fraught with pain its living,
It is a ladder tall,

That leads from earth to heaven,
From birth to endless life;
So why should I be craven
And shrink from pain and strife?

The Holy City's glory,
By God's abundant grace,
Shall be my only story,
Till there I find a place.
So ne'er again repining
For joys I may not share,
I will with face a-shining
Await my entrance there.

From the first little house to the last, the music of Pa Ingalls' fiddle resounded with happy songs and sad songs, songs of patriotism and songs of courage. Where Pa acquired the fiddle and his musical skill has always been a mystery, but the memories of the music Pa played always inspired his girls. Mary wrote a poem about what Pa's fiddle meant to her.

My Father's Violin

Long years have passed since childhood's happy day
Sorrow and joy have fallen in my way
Sunshine and shadow along my pathway lay
Happiness and misery have come and passed away
And rosy morn and twilight cold and gray

Never to fade and never to decay
Until this paper's page I print
With stylus of steel on slate of flint
The words which shall forever be
A record of the melody
That lifts my soul Oh God to thee.
Those sweet old strains shall ever rise
And be with me beyond the skies
Shall be with me and never die
Sweet strains of the "Sweet By and By,"
And oft the merry footsteps flew
And happy heart beats faster grew
As o'er the strings the bow he drew
And "Swanee River," "Home Sweet Home"
Shall be with me where e'er I roam
Through desert wild, o'er ocean foam
And make the glittering teardrop start
And faster beat the throbbing heart
But like some brilliant beacon star
As o'er the world I wander far
I seem to see my home again
My father and his violin.
Sweeter by far to my loving heart
Than minstrels of cultured art
Was music from those mystic strings
My father's hand to give it wings.
Oh how I wish for an hour once more

In that dear old home on Vermillion's* shore
How I long to enter that vine-wreathed door
And stand on that old familiar floor
Once more the dear ones there to greet
To think of the years that have passed so fleet
Since with childish romping feet
We roamed through the gardens and meadows sweet
And to look with many blinding tears
Into the vista of the coming years
What the future may bring we cannot know
Joy's wings are fleet, sorrow's are slow
Sorrow from joys of the present may glow
Or joy may come of our grief and woe
But ever and always the song in my heart
Shall be of the time when never to part
In the Heavenly home we'll meet again
Sanctified, glorified, cleansed from all sin.

The Ingalls family was so closely knit that any home—whether a covered wagon, log cabin, sod dugout, or claim shanty—seemed beautiful as long as they were all together. Mary's love of home and family was expressed in verse with special tenderness. Her reference to "sweet-faced little mother" recalls Ma's constant presence in Mary's life. After Pa's death, when the other girls had left De Smet, Ma and Mary were inseparable. "I am feet for Ma, and Ma is eyes for me," Mary explained. Sometimes they pined for the long-lost son and

---

* The Vermillion River, on which is the town of Vermillion, South Dakota.

brother, Charles Frederick Ingalls, who died in 1876 before he was a year old. "If only Freddie was here . . . ," they would say. In the following poem, Mary does not forget to mention the brother who might have become a strong support to lean upon, and indeed imagines a home in which all her loved ones are gathered together once again.

The Old Home

The summer sun is shining,
A disk of burnished gold,
For Home my heart is pining
With love of depth untold.
God grant me grace and power,
And grant a shining trail
To speed me home this hour;
O'er mountain, hill and vale.

The prairie rose is blushing
The sun's kiss on her cheek;
The wind with glee is rushing
In merry hide-and-seek.
The tiger lily's stalking
The gaudy goldenrod,
The meadow lark is talking
Of shadows on the sod.

The harvest moon is beaming
And casting silver sheen
Where life is hushed and dreaming
O'er field and meadow green.

Carrie, Mary, and Laura Ingalls posed for this tintype around 1880.

The far church bell is ringing
A-calling us to meet,
And join the throng a-singing
Our Saviour's praises sweet.

I long to see the homestead,
With trees a-shading o'er,
With roses in the garden bed
And sunshine on the floor;
The dear ones there a-dwelling
I long again to see,
And something keeps a-telling
A welcome's there for me.

The August sun is shining
A burnished disk of gold
My heart for home is pining—
The home I knew of old.
My sisters and my brother
For me are waiting there—
And sweet-faced little mother
With shining silver hair.

❀ Caroline Celestia Ingalls ❀

In 1930, Aubrey Sherwood, the energetic editor of The De Smet
News, *planned to commemorate the fiftieth anniversary of the
town and its newspaper with a massive edition of the town's history, including recollections of early settlers. He solicited the living
pioneers for their stories of homesteading, the Hard Winter, and
the growth of De Smet. The old-timers responded with amazing
detail. All were eager to tell tales and have them recorded in the
pioneer newspaper of Kingsbury County.*

Among the early settlers Editor Sherwood contacted were the Ingalls daughters. The Sherwoods and Ingallses had been neighbors, and both families belonged to the Congregational Church. Aubrey's grandfather, Samuel O. Masters, had also taught the Ingalls children in Walnut Grove, Minnesota.

For the golden anniversary edition of the News, Laura Ingalls Wilder contributed a poem, Grace Ingalls Dow wrote a history of the neighboring town of Manchester, and Carrie Ingalls Swanzey recounted her family's role in the settling of the community, which parallels her father's own account. Carrie was nine years old when she and her family moved to De Smet.

THE EARLY DAYS OF DE SMET

Father and Mother, Mr. and Mrs. C. P. Ingalls with their family, Mary, Laura, Grace and myself came to the C.&N.W. R.R.* construction camp on the banks of Silver Lake in 1879 where father was a timekeeper, bookkeeper and paymaster. This was the stretch of the R.R. grading from Brookings to De Smet. Trains came only to Tracy, Minn. From there we had to come overland in a spring buggy.

It was an ideal place for a camp for Silver Lake was a beautiful little lake full of water. This was probably why the surveyor's house was built on its bank.

I do not know anything about the working of the grading only it was done with horses and scrapers. I was not allowed to go far and never where the work was being done.

---

* Carrie was referring to the Chicago and Northwestern Railroad.

At night there would be a cloud of dust and the shouting men and trotting horses toward camp from work, which was the understood signal for me to go in. Then supper and bed.

But I do know there were some fine horses on the work, every man proud of his team, and often I remember father saying a good deal of rivalry about a team's ability, their knowledge of how to pull a scraper not to delay the line, and when the dump was coming and the style and grooming of the horses. It was no wonder that sometimes a horse thief picked a team. Sometimes a lone horseman would come out of the prairie, ride up and watch the grading work and ride away again into the prairie spaces, as they say, and that night the men would sleep with their teams.

One such horseman, wearing always a red shirt, big hat, and light trousers, and riding a white horse, not such a beautiful horse, but father remarked once "a mighty good one," when this horseman took a fancy to a horse or team they were just the same as gone, for he had the courage of his convictions and the nerve of a ——,* but I really don't know what a good horse thief has the courage of. I saw him riding through many times and to me he was great, but fearsome. There were many little things like this to make an impression on one's memory.

In the fall of 1879 when it was too late for the R.R. grading work the camp broke up and the surveyors went away,

---

* Carrie could not find the word she wanted and simply left an open space here.

but as they were to come back in the spring, they persuaded father and mother to stay and move into their house for the winter where they could leave the surveying outfit.

Father purchased their food supply which was quite a quantity. The only item I remembered was a large barrel with just about two layers of "hard tack" in the bottom which they said was not enough to count and I had my first and last taste of genuine hard tack. Memory has it that it was delicious.

Mr. R. A. Boast put up a house just a very little way, could not have been more than a hundred feet north of us; then brought Mrs. Boast there.

The folks often said the winter was mild, but I cannot recall about the snow or cold, I know we were all very comfortable. We two families spending the most of our evenings together. I used to go to sleep listening to father play songs, dance music, and hymns on his old violin or to the singing of hymns from that old "Pure Gold" hymn book which we all knew by heart before spring. It seemed a very happy time to me and looking back I know it must have been for the life-long friendship of the Boast and Ingalls families proved it.

Sometimes there were men traveling through and they always seemed so glad of a place to stop and always seemed to give the impression of coming from a long way off.

Mr. Boast often told of entertaining the people of De Smet and Lake Preston, for New Year's dinner. That was our family and a man who had taken a claim at Lake Preston but was staying at our house, nine in all.

Carrie Ingalls wrote "Burn this" on the back of this photograph, which shows her as a career woman in the early 1900's.

That was a lovely day, we ate dinner with the door open and after I had eaten all I could I left the others talking at the table and went out to play. . . .

As it got warmer the wild ducks and geese began to come, I remember early one morning there was such a noise, a din, it would be called, I ran out to see what it was. The lake was covered with wild geese, they were swimming and splashing and there were little waves on the lake, and every goose was talking. I was told they were choosing their mates for it was Valentine's Day and it was said birds chose their mates that day. That is how I remember the date. Mornings I used to watch the lake and with the wind blowing the water in little waves and the wild ducks and geese and quite a few times beautiful swans on its water. It was a sight no child could forget.

Spring came and with it the surveyors. Father used to go with them and one day he came home and said the town was all located. So after dinner I went to the top of the hill east of where the court house is now to see the "town" and all I saw was a lot of stakes in the ground. I went back and told mother there was nothing but sticks stuck in the ground and mother told me that where the stakes were would be houses and stores, a school house and a church.

Then in a little while we moved "to town," father putting up the house E. H. Couse bought for his first store. Then father built a house on the corner that Carroll bought for his bank.* This house was moved back quite a while later and is now C. L. Dawley's real estate office. My father, C. P. Ingalls

---

* This was the store building used as a residence by the Ingallses during the Hard Winter and during several later winters.

was first justice of the peace in Kingsbury County and the first justice court was held in the front room of our home.

Church services were also held there until the depot was put up, then the services were held there. Benches were made of boards, I certainly remember that. At that time there was just one other little girl my size in town. . . .

There was great joy and thoughtfulness and the lives of those early pioneers were bound together in an effort to build for the future not only a town, but a good town.

❀ Grace Pearl Ingalls ❀

Grace, the youngest Ingalls daughter, did what unfortunately the rest of the family did not: She kept a diary. As a nine-year-old, Grace started writing in a brown composition book, sporadically writing entries until 1893, when she turned sixteen. Her accounts include references to her parents and sisters; her niece, Rose Wilder; and her school life. Her spelling and punctuation are preserved.

FROM GRACE'S DIARY
Jan. 12th 1887. Tuesday.

Cousins Lee and Ella came to day with their baby Earl, they came with a covered wagon and a stove. I think Earl is real p[r]etty. He is just beginning to talk and say any thing you say. He thinks everything of Laura's baby and so do I. Thay stayed two weeks and then went away. Laura has a baby and it is just beginning to smile. It is eight weeks old, her name is Rose.

July 23 thursday.

It has just through raining we went down cellar too, the clouds looked so funny. My birthday was may 23 monday. I got the prettiest vase I ever saw, it's color gold. Then I got a birthday cake, it was frosted and had lemon drops on top.

Monday. March 5. 1888.

Today is warm but the ice is not melted. We live in town now in not a very large house but beter than the shanty. It has two rooms below and one overhead. We came hear the night before Christmas and it was the only plesant day for a long while. I have been to school all winter and am still going to Miss Master's I study Arithmetic, Reading, Spelling, Geography and Language. Our school-room is very nice. There are six windows, four of which have dark brown curtains or shades, the seates and desks are cullered a rose culler or very dark brown sutaibel for one schollar to sittin, the room is ornimated with pictures some with frames and some not. I like Miss Master's better and better. Laura and Manly were sick with diptheria and are just getting over it so we have Rose here. She is the best girl I ever saw. She can now say a good many words such as gramma and grampa and bread and butter and cracker.

April 13 1888

It has been a long while since I have written for it is spring and a very wet one. We have a storm calendar and there is a storm nearley every day marked on it. I lost a week

Grace Ingalls, probably around the turn of the century, when she was a rural schoolteacher near De Smet.

of school because I had the scarlet fever but no one knew it but us. School was closed on account of diptheria in town one little boy died with it. Miss Masters took the chance of the vaction and went and got married to Mr. Sherwood.* Miss Masters is a great deal taller than he so they must look funny together. Rose can walk nicely now she is broad as she

---

* Carter P. Sherwood, father of newspaper editor and historian Aubrey Sherwood.

is long. Carrie made two little cradels out of egg shells and gave one to Rose.

Tuesday August 27th 1889.

A great many things have happened since I last wrote in this book. Laura's little baby boy only a month old died a little while ago, he looked just like Manly. Rose will be three years old next december she is large for her age with golden hair and large blue eyes. Last friday Manly's house caught fire and burned to the ground. The furniture in the front room and in the bed room and pantry was saved but nothing in the kitchen where the fire started. Laura had just built a fire in their stove went into the other room and shut the door so she could sweep when the noise of the fire startled her and on opening the door she saw the roof and side of the kitchen was on fire . . . help came soon but they could not save the house and only some of their old clothing was saved they stayed down here for a while and then went to keep house for Mr. Sheldon one of their neighbors taking a hired girl with them.

Jan 2, 1890.

This is the second day of the new year and the first time I have written it. It seems not very long ago since I wrote 1889 for the first time and thought it looked so queer. We intended to celebrate this day by going to Mr. Boasts but it looked so stormy we did not. Christmas we had quite a good time. Mr. Boasts folks and Manlys folks were down. I got a lovly book it is Tenneson's Dora the cover looks like marble. Uncle Tom sent Mary a white silk handkerchief and ma and pa a picture of their two children Helen and Lillian they are both pretty. Carrie got a crazy work pin-cushion. We went to the tree and saw nothing but dolls. Carrie gave me my book and I can not find out how much it cost but I will yet though.

May 18. 1890

To day is Sunday it has eather been raining or blowing all day. We got all ready to go up to Laura's but it looked so like a storm we did not. They are going to Minn. Tuesday after next, going with a covered wagon and drive the stock they and Peter sold their flock of two hundred and twenty sheep to the butchers for five hundred dollars. They are going in a covered wagon Peter, Manly, Laura & Rose they will have it nice two a bed set up all the time in the wagon. Laura will have her pretty poney to ride on part of the time. This is a cold spring even now the last of may it is so cold we can not take the stove out of the front room. The plum trees are all in bloom they can be smelled half a mile away.

Sep. 3d 1893.

Am now sixteen years old. We still live in DeSmet and Carrie works on the same paper as before. Laura & Manly went to Florida came back and now live in DeSmet. Peter went to Florida married a girl down in that country. The Prof. is a man by the name of Ferrell he is irish, our old Prof.

Shannon went to Chicago & got married. I have not been well for almost a year have had Dr.'s Rice and Ensign. Mary went to Chicago last summer and had an operation for the neuralgia. Aunt Lillie and her two children, Aunt Eliza, and Aunt Martha visited with us last summer.

WRITING FROM THE PRAIRIE

For one who spent most of her life involved with the creative process of writing, Laura Ingalls Wilder was curiously silent about the fascination it held for her during her youth.

Silent though she may have been, the urge to capture her thoughts on paper was nonetheless always there. In fact, when her late-life career bloomed as the author of the Little House books, Laura was surprised to be hailed as a "newly discovered" writer. She had been discovering herself as a writer since those days on the Dakota prairie when she had first written poems in the backs of schoolbooks and on precious scraps of paper.

When Laura was sixteen, her instructor in the De Smet school was Professor V. S. L. Owen, a challenging, inspiring teacher who demanded the best from his students, and especially from the talented Laura Ingalls. "For Mr. Owen," Laura recalled, "I had written my first composition." The experience was significant. Laura preserved this first of what would become a lifetime of writings, and even incorporated it into her eighth Little House book, These Happy Golden Years. *She vividly recalled the details of the experience many years later.*

. . . [T]he subject was "Ambition." Not having been at school the day before, I did not know what was expected until a few minutes before recitation, when I found I was not prepared. The others had written their papers at home the night before.

I couldn't make a start, and in despair went to the

Laura Ingalls, age seventeen, as photographed by Cooledge, De Smet's pioneer photographer.

dictionary to see what it said about ambition, hoping to get an idea. I wrote my whole composition from the dictionary definition, closing with its quotation from Shakespeare, who I knew to be a great writer.

AMBITION

Ambition, like other good things, is good only when it is used in moderation. It has worked great good for the world and great evil also.

Alexander is an example of a man completely carried away by ambition: so much so that when he had conquered the whole world (which we would suppose was enough to satisfy ambition), he wept because there were no more worlds to conquer.

Ambition is a good servant, but a hard master; and if you think it is likely to become your master, I would say to you in the words of the immortal Shakespeare: "Cromwell, I charge thee fling away ambition, by that sin fell the angels."*

Mr. Owen looked at me sharply when I had finished reading it and said, "You have written compositions before."

"Oh no sir," I said. "This is my first."

"Well you should write more of them," said he. "I wouldn't have believed anyone could do so well the first time."

From this time on he often impressed upon Pa that every effort should be made to keep me in school as much of the term as possible and to give me every opportunity for an education.

While "Ambition" was Laura's first essay, what V. S. L. Owen did not know was that his prize student had been experimenting with

---

* Laura quoted from Shakespeare's *Henry VIII.*

her poetic voice since her family had settled down on their home-stead claim near De Smet. *Dakota Territory, in all its weather and moods and whims, provoked varied responses in those homesteaders who attempted to tame the new land. Some rhapsodized over the mystical sunrises and sunsets; others cursed the winds and the blistering sun. Laura commemorated the pioneer settlement of Dakota Territory as well as its tumultuous weather patterns in this poem, written sometime in the early 1880's when Laura was a teenager.*

A Wail from Dakota

Where the prairie winds unlimber,
Checked by neither hill nor timber;
Where but yesterday the coyote
Howled his minor-keyed ki-yi note;
Where but late in Sioux Indian story
Rode the plains in all their glory;
Where the lordly bison snorted,
And the antelope cavorted;
Where the wilderness unbroken
Of the future gave no token,
And geographers untruthful
Mapped out a desert ruthful;
Where might this be, you say?
'Twas Dakota, latter day.

Where from every land and nation
Throughout the wide creation;

Where from Poland's frozen mountains
To Italia's sunlit fountains;
Where from Kalamazoo to Sweden
Come seeking Mother Eve's lost Eden
Hither pushing, crowding, streaming,
Comes the world, gone mad in seeming,
Mecca of each pilgrim's aim,
Seeks fortune, health or fame;
Here contented rests the horde,
Thinking paradise restored.

But as luckless mortals never
From his lot all ill could sever,
Even here he fails to borrow
Absolute "surcease of sorrow"
Comes this wail from fair Dakota:
"Cut us loose from Minnesota."

O distress of mails belated!
Give us railroads elevated.
Heal our single imperfection
Give us underground connection
Through that cheerless region frigid,
Where all things seem lifeless rigid.

Where the snowdrifts piling higher
Emulates the tallest spire,
There the blizzard ceaseless howleth;

There the sullen north wind growleth
Thus becomes the winter dreary
Give us railroads to Dakota
Through our land but Minnesota.

In another, briefer poem, Laura wrote about the ever-present prairie winds, which blew ceaselessly for days and weeks at a time:

Voices

Listen to the voices of the wind:
Hear them howl and shriek and moan,
As if in pain;
Then sink, then rise and swell
The sad refrain:
Until we are enchanted,
Dreading yet longing,
To hear them again.

Grim prairie winters, with their frequent blinding blizzards and frigid temperatures, provided Laura with another poetic subject. When she wrote this poem, she had lived through the Hard Winter of 1880–1881, with its severe and endless blizzards. The final line of her poem, with its grim irony, perfectly captures the desperation of being pent up inside while storms roared outside.

The Ingalls homestead site near De Smet, as photographed by Garth Williams in 1947.

We remember not the summer
For it was long ago
We remember not the summer
In this whirling blinding snow
I will leave this frozen region
I will travel farther south
If you say one word against it
I will hit you in the mouth.

Laura perceived the simultaneously exhilarating and draining effect of land, sky, wind, and rain upon the people who lived on the broad plains. The immensity of the land both impressed and oppressed the settlers who came to Dakota. Some were able to survive and thrive; others wore down under the pressure of natural forces. In this poem, Laura mused on the sad quality of autumn time and the feelings of melancholy it produced in her.

A Comparison

The rain beats 'gainst the window pane
And drenches the withered grass;
And the sad winds wail a requiem,
O'er dead summer as they pass.

The trees have lost their beautiful leaves,
They lie on the ground below.
And they too are drenched in the falling rain,
And o'er them the sad winds blow.

My heart is full of withered hopes,
And it seems like rain to have bled,
While the winds of despair and passion
Howl a requiem o'er the dead.

The tree of my love has lost its leaves
Just as they were beginning to bud,
And now they are lying crushed and low
Drenched in the rain of blood.

When did Laura Ingalls begin experimenting with her poetic voice? No concrete evidence exists, but during the summer of 1881, when Laura was fourteen, national events inspired her comment. In July, a disgruntled office seeker shot and wounded President James A. Garfield, who died eighty days later. The assassination prompted Laura to write this poem.

Garfield! for whom all hearts
Have bled
All tongues showered curses
On the head
Of the low villain
Who would dare
To slay the president
Of this land so fair.

Perhaps the events leading to Garfield's death also inspired Laura to pen her thoughts on her country in this poem.

America

My country how I love thee
Land of the noble and the free
How my heart bounds within me
When thy true flag I see.

My heart does in rapture swell
At thought of the brave who fell
In woodland, field and dell
Fighting for thee.

Long may my country stand
The eagle's chosen land
Guarded by freedom's hand
Spotless and pure.

Laura's years at the De Smet school during the 1880's were her first concentrated educational experiences; never before had the Ingalls family been so near a school for so long. As a teenager, Laura learned more than books alone could offer. She discovered the fun of mingling with students her own age, as well as the pitfalls of cliques and quarrels among friends. Several poems were written during what she called the "reign" of schoolteacher Eliza Jane Wilder, who was Almanzo Wilder's sister and would become Laura's sister-in-law. These school traumas were described nearly sixty years later in Little Town on the Prairie, *but Laura wrote about those times as she lived them, too. This tongue-in-cheek poem depicts Laura's exasperation and rivalry with a fellow student in De Smet.*

The Difference

My neighbor and I
Can never agree
Kind reader be judge
Between her and me.

I go to the school
Which she attends
In which I have "chums"
And she has "friends."

She works "difficult problems"
While I do "hard sums"
She says it "continues"
While I say it "runs."

She thinks things are self-evident
That I think are true
I say it is "boss"
She says "too-too"

But this is the strangest of all
You will own
And shows quite a difference
When taken alone

That she banges her hair
While I bang my head
She "retires for the night"
While I "go to bed."

Laura's disdain for her teacher, which she clearly expresses in
Little Town on the Prairie, *is evident in this poem.*

I feel like a borned fool
For coming to this school
What is the use of coming here
Where there is no one to love or fear.
And:
Oh! I'll burst
If only I durst
I'd raise a row
I would I vow!

Following a misunderstanding at school, perhaps involving Laura's rival, Genevieve Masters, who was one of the models for Nellie Oleson, Laura wrote this poem.

A Lie

Of all mean things under the sun,
Telling a lie is the meanest one
By it, to three persons, injury is done,
To the lied to,
The lied about,
And to the liar, at least some.

It generally streaks many a good name
While nobody knows just who is to blame
And gives, not very enviable fame,
To the lied to,
The lied about
And the liar, the same.

Although school was often a topic for her poetry, Laura also wrote a number of poems that reveal the steady formation of her philosophies on life. This collection of brief maximlike poems expresses both her goal of living a sound moral life and her respect for a strong work ethic.

Do It with All Your Might

If you've anything to do,
Do it with all your might.
Don't let trifles hinder you,
If you're sure you're right.
Work away, work away,
Do it with all your might.

Hope

Hope on though storm clouds gather,
Hope on though hopes still die.
The darkest cloud will soon pass over,
The sun still reigns on high.

Little by Little

Little by little
The time flies by
Short if we laugh through it
Long if we sigh

Work

The work that is sweetest and dearest
The work that so many ne'er do
The great work of making folks happy
May be done by a lassie like you.

Ourselves

We think we know ourselves
But still we find
Where e'er we cast a curious glance behind
We have *not* known ourselves,
But *now* we say,
We surely know ourselves,
Yet ever 'tis the way
We are a puzzle to ourselves and all beside
And yet we are ourselves whate'er betide!

Laura also wrote poetry about her family. Mary, her elder sister, became the topic of a poem that captures both the differences between the two sisters and the deep devotion they shared.

My Sister Mary

Who is it shakes me
Like a Child
When e'er my spirits
Grow too wild
Who gives reproof in accents mild?
My sister Mary

Who is it trusts me
Without doubt
And ere she knows what
I'm about

Who will come quickly
to *help me out?*
My sister Mary

*As the oldest child at home in De Smet (Mary was in Iowa at the
school for the blind), Laura felt great responsibility to assist Pa
and Ma in their last attempt to create a successful farm, and to
prepare for a teaching job to bring in extra money to help pay for
Mary's education. Also, as a competitive student, Laura strove
hard to remain at the top of her class. The demands of life at home
and school led her to write this poem.*

Oh This Worry and Bother

Oh this worry, and bother, and fret,
This hustle, and bustle, and rush!
My head is all boiling and mixed,
Somewhat like a kettle of mush.

I am vexed with myself, and with you,
And with everyone under the sun,
It tires me to death, just to think
Of all that has got to be done.

I wish I could hasten away,
From this pace of turmoil and ill,
To some far away isle in the sea,
Where all is peaceful and still.

Where the waves slowly rise on the shore,
Then sink back again with a sigh,
And the only sound beside their murmur,
Is the sea bird's mournful cry.

Oh if there I might wander and dream,
I'd be willing to be called a shirk,
For I am so tired, of this
Hustle and hurry and work.

Laura was for the most part reticent and stoic; the Victorian era prescribed that women keep their emotions strongly checked. For Laura Ingalls, poetry clearly was an outlet for her to express her feelings, as she does in the poem above. So it is not surprising that Laura composed poetry throughout her early romance with Almanzo Wilder. Their courtship spanned the years 1883–1885, and Laura described it in These Happy Golden Years. *She told only part of the story in that book; her poetry, written during the courtship years, chronicled her growing consciousness of romance.*

Pride and Love
I angered my love and he rode away
In the twilight of evening cold and grey
And I waited and watched for him day by day
But he did not come.

Oh the time was weary, the days seemed long
I knew that I had been in the wrong
But love was weak, and pride was strong
And pride had won.

My love returned when a year was past
Close in his arms he held me fast
And any long watch was over at last
For he had come.

The days no longer seemed dull and long
But sped by so swiftly so full of song
For pride was weak, and love was strong
And love had won.

In 1884, Laura Ingalls and Almanzo Wilder were engaged; that fall, Almanzo and his brother Royal left De Smet on a long journey to the south. They drove a peddler's wagon filled with goods to trade as they traveled to the New Orleans Exposition. Laura was very lonely without her fiancé, and it is easy to imagine her sitting alone, writing love poetry to Almanzo. Her wait was shorter than she thought it would be; Almanzo made a surprise early return to De Smet, which is also described in These Happy Golden Years. *This poem celebrates Almanzo's return; the first line in the last stanza even puns on Laura's pet name for Almanzo, which was* Manly.

Laura and Almanzo Wilder as newlyweds.

So Far and Yet So Near

We're many miles apart my dear.
You're in a far strange place;
And many days will pass I fear,
Ere we meet face to face.

I can not look into your eyes
My hand you can not press;
You can not see my sorrow rise,
Nor smooth it by caress.

I miss you so since you have gone;
I'm lonely every day.
The weeks seem very long,
With you so far away.

You're far away and yet so near,
In word, and deed, and thought.
Your pleasant voice, I seem to hear
And feel the joy it brought.

I seem to hear your manly tread;
Your happy smile to see,
And distance loses half its dread;
You seem so near to me.

Laura also wrote this poem during Almanzo's absence.

The Call

Lonely! I am so lonely
Far from thee
Days come and go,
And are all the same
To me;
For thou, my beloved one
No more I see.
No more I hear thy footstep
Strong and free;
Nor meet thee, 'neath the scarlet
Maple tree.
Oh my beloved one! wherever
Thou mayest be,
Wandering on a foreign shore
Or on the sea,
Come, I recall thee
Home to me.

Almanzo was not himself a writer. His letters to Laura were brief and irregular. But Laura imagined Almanzo's return to her, perhaps riding over the low prairie hill where she waited in Pa's claim shanty. So Laura wrote the reply she longed for.

The Reply

Love I am coming
For far o'er the ocean
I heard thy heart
Calling to mine;
And with joy over-flowing,
O'er the wild waves' commotion,
My heart is replying,
To thine.

THE HOUSE ON
ROCKY RIDGE FARM

"Home" had always been a word of irony for Laura Ingalls Wilder; for her family, a permanent home had been a much-desired but seldom-achieved goal. Finally, after ten years of journeying through the woods and prairies, the Ingalls family settled in De Smet, Dakota Territory. After her marriage in 1885, Laura knew the satisfaction of living in a house her husband had built with his own hands. Her comfort was short-lived, however; the "little gray home in the west" went up in flames in August 1889. After that, there were more years of living in temporary rented homes and with relatives.

At long last, though, after buying Rocky Ridge Farm near Mansfield, Missouri, Laura and Almanzo started to plan their dream home. It began with an addition to their one-room log cabin home in the spring of 1895. The building site then shifted to the top of the Ozark knoll that crested their farm. With starts and stops, the construction continued over eighteen years, including a stint living in a house in the village of Mansfield. Finally, in 1913, the Wilders' home was completed. The local newspaper, The Mansfield Mirror, *noted in its September 25, 1913, issue that "A. J. Wilder is building a fine residence on his farm near Mansfield. Mr. Wilder is one of our most progressive farmers."*

The Rocky Ridge farm became one of Laura's favorite topics to write about, and indeed, it was as an expert farmwife that Laura first began earning money for her writing. In this article,

Laura describes the hilarious and sometimes hair-raising process of building her final home, and at the same time, she gives us an amusing and loving portrait of her marriage to Almanzo. Laura teasingly referred to Almanzo as "The-Man-Of-The-Place," although in truth, he deferred to his wife's every whim in the construction of the house that became the home where the Little House books were written.

THE BUILDING OF A FARM HOUSE

The house on Rocky Ridge Farm is the result of evolution. It has come through slow development from the one room log house, with shake roof, slab door and overgrown fireplace that we found on the farm when we came to it.

The light in the log house, what there was of it, came down the chimney and through holes in the mud chinking between the logs of the walls. If, for any reason, we needed more light, we just punched out some more of the chinking. It could easily be replaced with a handful of mud if the wind should blow in too cold as it frequently did, for the suction of that large chimney drew the cold air in through all the cracks, so that sitting with one's feet on the hearth before a blazing fire, the chills would creep up and down one's back.

When spring came, we added a box room with doors and windows to the log room and the next year we took the new room, leaving the log one behind us, moved to a different building site and built an addition of one room. We were very proud of our two-roomed box house, but regretted the fireplace and at times would plan to build another.

The emerging farmhouse under construction.

At last came a time when The-Man-Of-The-Place proposed that we add another box room with a stairway, a loft and a fireplace. He could get most of the materials from the farm, he said, so it would not be very expensive.

But someway the idea did not appeal to me. I could do very well with two boxes, but two were enough. As usual when we disagree, The-Man-Of-The-Place and I talked it out. There was material on the farm to build any kind of a house, I argued, so why not build a real house instead of an addition that would make it look like a town house in the poorer suburbs? That kind didn't belong on a farm, I insisted. It wouldn't look right among the trees, with the everlasting hills around it.

I can't tell you what The-Man-Of-The-Place argued. Fact is I didn't listen to it and so, of course, I had my way. "Draw the plans," said he, and then I learned that there was quite some difference between drawing on my imagination for a house and drawing it on paper, but draw the plans I did, though with much chewing of tongue and pencil.

So far as possible, everything used in the building was to be a product of the farm, both for the sake of economy and because of the sentimental idea that we wanted the house actually to be a part of the farm. To be sure the lumber was still growing in the oak trees and the rocks for foundations and chimneys were scattered over the fields. But, "A difficulty raiseth the spirit of a man" and we accepted its challenge with good hearts.

Logs were cut in the timber; hauled to mill; sawed into dimension stuff and boards and piled neatly to season. Although at that time, I had never seen a beamed ceiling, I wanted one, so large beams were sawed out and stacked to dry so that they would not twist.

We let the lumber and timbers season, for a year, and then early in the spring we began building. We were to use one of the old rooms for the kitchen in the new house and raise the roof to the same height, one and a half stories. In front of this was to be one large room, subdivided, and along the south side an extension for a bedroom and an office. The other old room was to be a woodshed behind the kitchen.

Until you have had a house built over your head, you can not appreciate the things that happened to us that summer.

Unless you have struggled with the ignorance and independent touchiness of country workmen in their native wilds, you never will know what all we had to put up with to get the work done at all.

The carpenter insisted that he couldn't frame the building until the foundation was built to put it on, while the stonemason swore, literally, that he couldn't put a foundation under a building until the building was there to put it under. It seemed likely to be a new version of which was first, the acorn or the oak, but finally they compromised, the mason laying the corner stones while the carpenter fitted the sills and then the mason worked under the sills while the carpenter put up the rest of the frame.

Then came the unroofing of the old room so that the whole roof might be made at once. Of the two old rooms, one was the kitchen, pantry and separator room and it was small. The other was also small and filled with the bed, the organ, the writing desk and chairs. Over it was a small loft, reached by a ladder, and there I kept our few clothes to which I had just added a new spring dress and hat.

The roof had to come off, but I could not move the things downstairs, for I had to keep enough room in which to feed the workmen, as is the lot of country women, so I laid the clothes on the low couch in the center of the attic floor, put my new hat on top and covered all carefully with a waterproof cloth to keep off dust and moisture, for it would be several days before the roof would be replaced. I warned the workmen to keep off the pile as there was plenty of room for them to work around it.

And that night it rained! It didn't wait even until the next

One of the sentinel oaks near Rocky Ridge Farmhouse, 1925. Huge trees like this one provided timber for the construction of the house.

day! In the night I heard the rain and then I thought it stopped, but it had turned to snow instead, the last, late flurry of the spring.

As soon as possible in the morning, I went up the ladder to shake the snow off my one good dress and my new hat. Imagine my dismay when I saw that the carpenters had thrown all the pieces of old lumber on the couch. That, with the clothes and my hat in the middle of it made a firm foundation for the pile of scraps that had been torn off the roof. There was this to be said—The snow hadn't damaged the hat any.

Between discussions with the carpenters and farm work, The-Man-Of-The-Place hauled rocks from the fields to build the chimneys. Foundations for the fireplace chimney were sunk four feet below the surface of the ground on a cement foundation base. To build the chimney, it took forty loads of rock, twenty-five hundred pounds of cement, seven barrels of lime and several loads of sand. Completed it is three feet, three inches by seven feet at its base and twenty-eight feet high above the ground. In the wall of it, at a good height to be easily seen, we laid numbers of curious rock formations, that we had picked up in the fields, some of which had lain at the bottom of the seas on that far past day when their waters covered the land that is now the Ozark Hills.

I had set my heart on having the fireplace made of rock off the farm, but The-Man-Of-The-Place had become tired of hauling rocks and to my consternation returned from town one day with a load of fire bricks to use instead. I

The rock chimney included native fossils and odd rock formations.

objected strenuously; I argued; I begged; I declared that if it was too much work to build the fireplace as it should be then we would have none but would use a heater. And at last, when everything else failed I wept. For the only time in my life, I made use of woman's time-honored weapon, tears, and to my surprise it worked. The fireplace was built of one enormous slab of rock across the whole length of the top and one at each end forming the whole end of the fireplace. The rock across the top is four feet three inches long and is fifteen and one half inches across the flat face of it above the supporting rocks at the ends. These three rocks make the fireplace which is four feet three inches wide, four feet ten inches high, three feet deep and extends into the room seven inches. The hearth is made of cement. The rocks are cool in the summer and help to keep the room from being too warm, but after there has been a fire for a few days, they as well as the cement hearth become heated through and stay so day and night. This makes an even, steady heat in the room that keeps it and the upstairs around the open stairway, comfortably warm. Above the fireplace is a heavy, polished oak mantleshelf.

We planned to have a part of the living room cut off by a paneling four and one-half feet high, with two doorways to be formed by posts eight by eight inches, reaching from the floor to a large beam in the ceiling.

We carefully explained to the carpenter, giving measurements, then left him with the work, to find later that he had made the paneling two feet high and the posts, resting on top of the paneling instead of on the floor, only three inches by four. He said he would not make it as we had told him, because he could not afford to ruin his reputation by building such a house. Then we found he had driven and clinched a nail in the face board of the stairway. Of this he said that it didn't matter, it was such a rough job anyway, so we stopped and rested.

It was a rough job, no mistake. The oak lumber came from the little country sawmill rough sawed and had to be dressed by hand. The carpenter could not plane it smooth, for it took a certain know-how which he lacked. We had expected a good deal of him and he had failed.

After some time, we found back in the woods a man who worked at carpenter work now and then. His father had been an old time wagon maker when the work had all been done by hand and he had carefully trained his son, when the learning of a trade meant using the brains as well as the hands. This man did not claim to be an experienced carpenter, but said he would do the work if we would tell him how we wanted it done.

It was late summer before he began and through the fall and winter, he and The-Man-Of-The-Place worked amiably together. He could smooth the beautiful oak boards so that they would take a fine finish; he could fit boards together until the joining could not be seen and he made the paneling and posts, shelves and stairway where and as we wanted them.

This backwoods carpenter, with the old-fashioned training was always courteous and willing and so at last the house was finished, just a year from the time we began to build; two years from the time we sawed the trees down to make the lumber.

While building the house, we had kept the farm work going so that we were able from it to meet the bills as they came due and by using our own materials as far as possible and our own labor wherever we could, we had built, for twenty-two hundred dollars, a house that would have cost us five thousand if it had been built in the usual way. And being built of good material, with painstaking hand work it has kept in good condition and today could not be replaced for less than eight thousand dollars.

The living room is fourteen by twenty-four feet in size, with the fireplace in the center of the north wall. The walls are paneled three feet and a half high and above this is wall board finished in dark oak color, also paneled.

The open stairs at the south end of the room have a

landing four steps up and turn here at right angles. On the landing is a door leading to my office. All the woodwork is solid oak finished in the natural color. The large windows, with the oaken window seats under them, frame wonderful views of woodland and hills and the effect is not marred by the curtains. They hide none of the windows.

On the east side, extending the whole length and really a part of the living room, being separated from it only by the paneling, is a room nine feet wide. This is divided again into two parts, the north part being shelved and filled with books, called by courtesy the library; the south part is really a small hall giving passage to the dining room, but as the organ and victrola are there we call it the music room.

The wall board above the book shelves and in the music room is old ivory in color. It blends with the coloring of the living room, the oak carrying many tones of browns and tans and yellows. The floor is dark brown and my rugs are brown and tan. The room might perhaps be too brown but for the sunshine through the windows bringing out the golden tints and the white of the under window curtains and touches of blues and yellows in the cushions scattered here and there. All together, the living room strikes the key note of color for the house, the coloring in any other room being a development of some tone found here. The effect is particularly good in summer when all the doors are open, making all the different parts of the house a harmonious whole.

From the living room one can look over the paneling and out through the window of the library onto the north

An early photograph of the parlor.

porch and into the branches of a walnut tree. This with the arrangement of the three rooms being really one, of the open stairs, the uncovered windows and the unobstructed view from the front door, through the wide doorway between the large posts into the music room, through the door from there into the dining room and on, into and through the kitchen, to the outdoors beyond its windows and glass door, gives an effect of light and spaciousness that is beautiful.

This appearance caused me to receive a rather dubious compliment from a photographer who came to take pictures of the place. "Your house is beautiful," said he, "it is so clean."

One neighbor, who came to see the house, looked up at the oak beams of the ceiling, seven by nine inches large, resting at each end on a larger beam along the sides of the room, the one on the east ten by sixteen inches, supported by the

Laura, Almanzo, and their dog in front of the completed farmhouse.

posts eight by eight inches of the doorways into the library
and music room. After gazing at them for some time he
grunted, "Must have thought she was building a mill."

Another neighbor, after looking around silently for a few
moments, said "I like your house, it is not so—so—" and after
struggling for a word to fit he repeated, "I like your house, it
is not so monotonous."

But my dear friend said, "You have expressed yourself! It
fits you as though it were your shell."

As I said before, the house on Rocky Ridge Farm is an
evolution, a growth from a small beginning. Made almost
entirely of materials from the farm, it seems to belong on the
low hill where it stands, with the tree covered mountain at
its back.

When the big farmhouse on Rocky Ridge was complete, the Wilders filled it with guests. Through the years, their home was known for its hospitality. Guests mingled in the rooms for many events; club meetings, socials, dances, costume parties, card parties, dinner, and drop-ins. Some came for extended stays on the Wilder farm, generally during the summer months. Those were the days when doctors prescribed summers in the country and changes of air for difficult-to-treat patients. Long visits were also somewhat determined by the fact that transportation was slow and tedious. Laura's summer boarders were both friends and paying guests, and often the paying guests became friends. One young boy named Julian Bucher spent a summer on Rocky Ridge. He became devoted to Laura and remained in contact with her even when he left Mansfield and became a businessman in Kansas City. In this article, Laura tells of the Wilder hospitality, and gives some practical advice to farmwives considering ways to make a bit of extra money.

SUMMER BOARDERS

There is one crop that the women on the farm can be reasonably sure of harvesting, no matter how hot the weather—in fact, the hotter and dryer the weather the greater this yield—and that is the crop of summer boarders.

When the hot season comes people in the cities think longingly of green fields, shady nooks and cool running water and if possible go in search of these pleasant things. Then is the opportunity for us to have a pleasant change from the monotony of farm life and also to earn a tidy sum which we can spend if we please in a trip to the city next winter.

If you have some spare rooms in your house by all means fill them with summer boarders and try marketing some of your surplus farm products that way. Get help in the kitchen if you can but if not, put out the washing, buy the bread and make the work light in every way you can.

Do not try to give them their meals in city style. They have come to the country for the sake of living the country life for awhile. Your common every-day things will be treats to them. Newly laid eggs, thick sweet cream, new milk, fresh buttermilk and butter, the fruits and vegetables fresh from the garden, are things nearly impossible to get in the city.

These things cost next to nothing on the farm and with the addition of some of the frying chickens are nearly all that is needed to make a delightful bill of fare for the summer. Everything necessary for the most delicious salads is ready at hand and they are not difficult to make although this is a dish too often neglected in the country.

The using of the things raised on the farm, many of which would otherwise go to waste or be sold at small price, is where the profit will be made and it will also give the greatest satisfaction to the summer visitors.

The first time I took summer boarders a couple of my friends began at the same time. I followed this idea of using home products and made a good profit from the start, doing better as I learned from experience. My friends could make no profit and even lost money.

The difference was that they bought fancy meats and canned goods. If they planned a salad they made a fruit salad

Laura in her daily housewife garb, on the porch of the Wilder house in Mansfield. She wore this housedress when preparing meals for the railroad workers and was possibly caught unawares, because she penciled on the back of this photo, "Just as I am, without one plea."

of pineapple, bananas, oranges, etc., while I went to the garden where I gathered tender lettuce, which arranged on pretty plates with a hard boiled egg cut in half to show the golden center and a little ball of cottage cheese made a beautiful and tasty salad. The dressing for the salads I made myself of homemade cider vinegar, mustard, sugar, an egg, with pepper and salt. When my friends prepared a dessert it was some expensive pudding or pastry while I served fresh berries, peaches or other fruit with sugar and cream.

The result was that while I made money they lost it and the humor of the situation was that their boarders wanted to leave them and come to me.

By using home products in this way, combining with them a spirit of hospitality, a little taking of thought and some extra steps you can receive in return at least $5 a week and often more for each person entertained, and fully half of this will be profit.

I make it a plan, each week when the board money is paid, to set aside exactly half the sum to pay for my work, leaving the rest to pay the expenses of the following week. With the farm to draw on for supplies, I have never had to draw on my half, and often have found I did not require the entire sum set out for expenses.

However, a well set table is not all that is necessary to make the summer boarder eager to come back next season and bring his friends. Of course everything about the house must be kept spotlessly clean. The windows should be well screened as well as the doors, and ceaseless war must be waged on flies. By darkening the house in the early morning and leaving one door on the sunny side of the house open, a few minutes with a towel or apron will drive out the few flies that managed to slip in the day before, and make it unnecessary to have sticky fly paper and poison setting around.

Be sure to have the beds comfortable. This usually means a new mattress or two, for I have yet to find the summer boarder who liked either a feather bed or a straw tick.

Another great convenience is a large closet or even a little unused shed which is fitted up as a bathroom. If there is no system of running water in the farm house, put a tub, plenty of towels, soap and a large jar of water in this place, ready for use at any time. This is one of the little points that make it pleasant for your guests.

One reason country women hesitate to take boarders from the city is fear of being "looked down on" because they live in the country and take boarders. Speaking from my own experience I have never found this so and have always been treated with the greatest consideration. Some of my dearest friends are among the people whom I first met in this way.

I think we receive a great deal what we expect in this world and if we meet the stranger at the door with the feeling, "Don't you dare to feel above me" we are bound to show that feeling in some way and are taken at our own valuation, which is less than it should be or the thought would never enter our minds that we might be considered inferior.

Of course we will meet people in this way whom we will not care for and who will not care for us, but we should meet them all with the hospitality and consideration we would show to guests. Never try to make them members of the family. They will not like this and neither will you. Remember they have come to the country to rest and leave them to their own devices most of the time, providing delicious food, good beds, and friendly companionship when they seek it.

In this way keeping summer boarders proves a success for the country women, financially, mentally and socially.

THE MISSOURI RURALIST YEARS

Farm families were often many miles away from agencies and information sources that could help them keep abreast of new agricultural developments and news. Farm-oriented newspapers and bulletins helped the Wilders to perfect farming techniques and to feel a kinship with thousands of other small-scale farmers across the land. For Laura, rural journalism also became an important first step into the world of publication.

Laura's poultry advice columns and miscellaneous articles on agricultural topics first appeared in print in the early 1900's in the Star Farmer, *a publication based in St. Louis. Her first byline was "Mrs. A. J. Wilder."*

Laura soon found she had more to discuss with country readers than egg production and gardens. In February 1911, she began a long association with the Missouri Ruralist, *which would lead her to experiment with a variety of literary genres: essays, interviews, poetry, feature stories, and editorials on current events.*

From 1911 to 1915, Laura's work appeared only a handful of times in the Ruralist, *which was one of several farm weeklies published by Arthur Capper's syndicate. But then, Laura's trip to the San Francisco World's Fair in 1915 turned into something of a literary watershed for her. After she had reported on agriculture-related topics from the Fair,* Ruralist *editor John Case finally took special notice of the woman from Rocky Ridge Farm in Mansfield and asked her to contribute more regularly. By 1916, Laura's work was appearing twice monthly. This pace continued until*

1919, when a special column called "The Farm Home" was created for her. In 1921, the column was retitled "As a Farm Woman Thinks."

Details of Laura's career with the Missouri Ruralist *are sketchy; since the publication was a weekly newspaper, no one thought of its content as lasting literary material. Laura saved little correspondence from these years, but she clearly earned the respect of John Case and George F. Jordan, her editors. The latter wrote the following note to her in 1921:*

> *This is rather a long letter for an overworked editor, but I don't write you often—and I wanted to let you know that with your stories the pleasure of reading them compensates the hatred I have of editing and proofreading. Frankly, Mrs. Wilder, I like you and your stories better than anything which reaches us. That's more of a compliment than you may realize—but withal there is no flattery here—it's just a little confession of my likes. . . .*

Laura's association with the Missouri Ruralist *brought her a small but steady income, which was a welcome addition to the sometimes-meager returns of Rocky Ridge Farm. She was probably paid in space rates, a system by which columns were measured and recompensed by the inch. Steady checks for $2.50, $5, and $7.50 assured Laura that writing for the publication was a paying proposition. With some of her early earnings, she purchased a typewriter and thereafter submitted her work typed, on half-sheets of yellow paper.*

During her Ruralist *years, Laura sometimes wrote of pioneering days—her family's and those of friends she met in the Ozarks. The frontier experience she had known as a child left its imprint, and Laura was eager to share those early days with readers. Interestingly, Laura considered the building of an Ozark farm as much a pioneering experience as the establishment of a homestead on the prairie. She and Almanzo had carved out Rocky Ridge Farm from the wilderness, and she delighted in stories of Ozark neighbors who had done the same, frequently using them as the basis of articles. In "A Homemaker of the Ozarks," published in the June 20, 1914, issue of the* Missouri Ruralist, *Laura recounts the experience of a farming neighbor, Mrs. C. A. Durnell, and her daughter, Priscilla; this article, like many of Laura's other writings, quietly praises the values of common sense and thrift.*

A HOMEMAKER OF THE OZARKS

Women have always been the homemakers, but it is not usually expected of them that they should also be the home builders from the ground up. Nevertheless they sometimes are and their success in this double capacity shows what women can do when they try. Among the women who have done both is Mrs. C. A. Durnell of Mansfield, Missouri. She has not only made a home but she has put a farm in condition to support it.

Mansfield is on the very crest of the Ozarks and the land is rough and hilly, covered with timber, where it has not been cleared. Although one of the most beautiful places in the world to live, with a soil repaying bountifully the care given it, still it is no easy thing to make a farm out of a piece of the rough land. Imagine then the task for a woman, especially one with no previous experience of farming.

Mrs. Durnell was a city woman and for twenty years after her marriage, lived in St. Louis where her husband worked in the railroad terminal yards. Here she raised her three children until the eldest, a son, was through college and established in his profession.

None of the children were strong and about this time the second, a daughter, was taken sick with consumption, while the youngest, also a daughter, was threatened with the same disease. Hoping to restore their health, Mrs. Durnell brought them into the Ozarks, but too late to save the sick daughter.

As the other daughter showed signs of improvement, Mrs. Durnell decided to stay and the thought came to her to go on a little farm and make a home for her own and her husband's old age.

Sickness and the expense of living had used up the most of Mr. Durnell's wages as they went along and all they had to show for their twenty years of work was a house with a mortgage on it. Mrs. Durnell saw what so many do not realize until too late, that when Mr. Durnell became too old to hold his position any longer they would have no business of their own and quite likely no home either. A small farm, if she could get one running in good shape, would be a business of their own and a home where they could be independent and need not fear the age limit.

Mr. Durnell stayed with his job in St. Louis, to be able to

MISSOURI RURALIST

Vol. XIII, No. 12   JUNE 20, 1914   Fifty Cents a Year

A Homemaker of the Ozarks

Mrs. Durnell Reclaimed a Farm, Built a House in the Wilderness and Learned the Secret of Contentment

BY MRS. A. J. WILDER
Editor Home Department, Mansfield, Mo.

WOMEN have always been the home makers, but it is not usually expected of them that they should also be the home builders from the ground up. Nevertheless they sometimes are and their success in this double capacity shows what women can do when they try. Among the women who have done both is Mrs. C. A. Durnell of Mansfield, Mo. She has not only made a home but she has put a farm in condition to support it.

Mansfield is on the very crest of the Ozarks and the land is rough and hilly, covered with timber, where it has not been cleared. Although one of the most beautiful places in the world to live, with a soil repaying beautifully the care given it, still it is no easy thing to make a farm out of a piece of the rough land. Imagine then the task for a woman, especially one with no previous experience of farming.

Mrs. Durnell was a city woman and for twenty years after her marriage, lived in St. Louis, where her husband worked in the railroad terminals until the eldest, a son, was through college and established in his profession.

None of the children were strong and about this time the second, a daughter, was taken sick with consumption, while the youngest, also a daughter, was threatened with the same disease. Hoping to restore their health, Mrs. Durnell brought them into the Ozarks, but too late to save the sick daughter.

As the other daughter showed signs of improvement, Mrs. Durnell decided to stay and the thought came to her to go on a little farm and make a home for her own and her husband's old age.

Sickness and the expense of living had used up the most of Mr. Durnell's wages as they went along and all they had to show for their twenty years of work was a home with a mortgage on it. Mrs. Durnell saw what so many do not realize until too late, that when Mr. Durnell became too old to hold his position any longer they would have no business of their own and quite likely no home either. A small farm, if she could get one running in good shape, would be a business of their own and a home where they could be independent and need not fear the age limit.

Mr. Durnell started with his job in St. Louis, to be able to send what money he could spare to help in making the start.

They secured a farm of 40 acres a quarter of a mile from town. Ten acres was in an old, worn-out field that to use a local expression had been "farmed to death"; 5 acres was in an old orchard, unkempt, neglected and grown up to wild blackberries. In the thick hills, neglected ground will grow up to wild blackberry briars, loaded with fruit in season. As the shiftless farmer said, "anyone can raise blackberries if he will not too farmed lazy." Aside from this

old orchard and the worn-out field, the place was covered with oak thicket where the land had been cleared and then allowed to go back. This second growth of oak was about six feet high and as large around as a man's wrist. The fences were mostly down and such as were standing were the old worm, rail fence. The house was a log shack.

Mrs. Durnell and her daughter moved into the log house and went to work. They bought a cow to furnish them milk and butter, but the cow would not stay inside the tumble-down fences, so repairing the fence was the first job. Some of it they built higher with their own hands and some they hired rebuilt, but there was only a little money to go on, so the work moved slowly. When the fences were in order and the cow kept at home they felt that a great deal had been gained.

The property in St. Louis was sold and after paying the mortgage there was enough left to build a five room house, which Mr. Durnell planned and the construction of which she superintended. It was a happy day for them when they moved from the log cabin into the comfortable new house, although it stood in a thick patch of the oak thicket that made them feel terribly alone in the wilderness.

The crop the first year was 150 gallons of wild blackberries which grew in the orchard. There were no apples.

In the spring, Mrs. Durnell hired the 10 acre field broken; then she and the daughter planted it to corn.

Swinging the Old-Fashioned Cradle.

When the corn was large enough to be cultivated, a neighbor boy was hired to plow it and when he said the job was done she paid him for plowing the 10 acres. What was her surprise, some time later when walking across the field, to find that only ten rows on the outside of the field had been plowed and the rest was standing waist high in weeds. Since then she has personally overseen the work on the place.

Mrs. Durnell was learning by experience also and was studying farming with the help of good farm papers and the state university and experiment stations. By the second spring she had learned better than to continue planting corn on the old field, so that spring she sowed it to oats and in the fall put it in wheat with a generous allowance of fertilizer. With the wheat was sowed 8 pounds of timothy

seed to the acre and the next February 6 pounds of clover seed to the acre was sown over the field. When the wheat was cut the next summer there was a good stand of clover and timothy. The field was so rocky and brushy however that no one would cut the hay so the grass was wasted. This naturally suggested the next thing to be done, and the brush was sprouted out and the stones picked up, so that the grass could be cut; and the crop of hay secured.

A good many men have failed to raise alfalfa, in the hills, but Mrs. Durnell has succeeded. She says that certo in preparing a good seedbed and plenty of fertilizer does the trick. The ground must be rich and the soil worked and fitted it before alfalfa seed is sown, she says. One piece was sown in April and another was sown in September; both are a success.

The whole place is now cleared and seeded to grass, except in a little draw, where the timber is left to shade and protect the springs and where the garden and berries grow.

Mrs. Durnell and her daughter cleared away some of the oak thicket and set out blackberries, raspberries, strawberries and grapes for home use. The wild blackberries have been transplanted, the ground cultivated and seeded to grass. Now there are plenty of apples and good grass for hay instead of wild blackberries and briars.

Gardening has been carefully studied; and the garden is always planned to raise the greatest variety and amount possible on the ground, and with the least labor. It is planted so long rows so that it can be plowed and have very little hand work. A furrow is plowed the length of the garden to plant the Irish potatoes in. These are dropped and lightly covered. This leaves them a little lower than the rest of the ground. As they are cultivated the dirt is thrown toward them and when they are cultivated for the last time they are hilled up and the weeds have been kept down, all without any hand work. At the last cultivation, kafir and milo are planted between the rows of potatoes and early garden stuff and there is plenty of time for it to mature and make fine large heads of grain for chicken feed.

Of all on her farm Mrs. Durnell is most interested in her flock of beautiful Rhode Island Reds. "I love them because they are so bright," she says, and they certainly seem to appreciate her kindness. Although they all look alike to a stranger, she knows every one by sight and calls them pet names as they feed from her hand. She knows which pullets lay the earliest and saves their eggs for hatching, for she has made a study of poultry as well as the other branches of farming, and knows that in this way she improves the laying qualities of the flock. "When starting my flock," said Mrs. Durnell, "I determined to have the best and I still get the best stock obtainable." She selects her breeders very carefully both for their early laying qualities and for their color and makes a flock *(Continued on Page 6.)*

White the Durnells First Lived.   Mrs. Durnell and her Poultry.   The House a Woman Built.

The lead story in one issue of the Missouri Ruralist *in 1914 was Laura's article about Mrs. Durnell. The photograph on the upper right shows Laura and Rose in the ravine behind the Rocky Ridge farmhouse.*

send what money he could spare to help in making the start.

They secured a farm of 23 acres a quarter of a mile from town. Ten acres were in an old, wornout field that to use a local expression had been "corned to death". Five acres were blackberries. In the Ozark hills, neglected ground will grow up to wild blackberry briars, loaded with fruit in season. As the shiftless farmer said, "anyone can raise blackberries if he aint too durned lazy." Aside from this old orchard and the wornout field the place was covered with oak thicket where the land had been cleared and then allowed to go back. This second growth oak was about six feet high and as large around as a man's wrist. The fences were mostly down and such as were standing were the old worm, rail fence.* The house was a log shack.

Mrs. Durnell and her daughter moved into the log house and went to work. They bought a cow to furnish them milk and butter, but the cow would not stay inside the tumble-down fences, so repairing the fence was the first job. Some of it they built higher with their own hands and some they hired rebuilt, but there was only a little money to go on, so the work moved slowly. When the fences were in order and the cow kept at home they felt that a great deal had been gained.

The property in St. Louis was sold and after paying the mortgage there was enough left to build a five room house,

---

* A worm fence is made up of several layers of wooden rails laid one on top of the other. Each layer is put down at a slightly different angle from the one below it, so that the fence, when finished, zigzags across the ground like an earthworm.

which Mr. Durnell planned and the construction of which she superintended. It was a happy day for them when they moved from the log cabin into the comfortable new house, although it stood in a thick patch of the oak thicket that made them feel terribly alone in the wilderness.

The crop the first year was 154 gallons of wild blackberries which grew in the orchard. There were no apples.

In the spring, Mrs. Durnell hired the ten acre field broken; then she and the daughter planted it to corn. When the corn was large enough to be cultivated, a neighbor boy was hired to plow it and when he said the job was done she paid him for plowing the ten acres. What was her surprise, when walking across the field, to find that only ten rows on the outside of the field had been plowed and the rest was standing waist high in weeds. Since then she has personally overseen the work on the place.

Mrs. Durnell was learning by experience, also she was studying farming with the help of good farm papers and the state university and experiment stations. By the second spring she had learned better than to continue planting corn on the old field, so that spring she sowed it to oats and in the fall put it in wheat with a generous allowance of fertilizer. With the wheat was sowed 8 pounds of timothy seed to the acre and the next February 6 pounds of clover seed to the acre was sown over the field. When the wheat was cut the next summer there was a good stand of clover and timothy. The field was so rocky and brushy however that no one would cut the hay so the grass was wasted. This naturally suggested the next thing to be done, and the brush was sprouted out and the stones picked up, so that the grass could be cut; and the crop of hay secured.

A good many men have failed to raise alfalfa, in the hills, but Mrs. Durnell has succeeded. She says that care in preparing a good seedbed and plenty of fertilizer does the trick. The ground must be rich and the weeds must be worked out of it before alfalfa seed is sown, she says. One piece was sown in April and another was sown in September; both are a success.

The whole place is now cleared and seeded to grass, except in a little draw, where the timber is left to shade and protect the spring; and where the garden and berries grow.

Mrs. Durnell and her daughter cleared away some of the oak thicket and set out blackberries, raspberries, strawberries and grapes for home use. The wild blackberries have been cleaned out of the orchard, the apple trees have been trimmed, the ground cultivated and seeded to grass. Now there are plenty of apples and good grass for hay instead of wild blackberries and briars.

Gardening has been carefully studied; and the garden is always planned to raise the greatest variety and amount possible on the ground, and with the least labor. It is planted in long rows so that it can be plowed and leave very little to hand work. A furrow is plowed the length of the garden to plant the Irish potatoes in. These are dropped and lightly covered. This leaves them a little lower than the rest of the ground. As they are cultivated the dirt is thrown toward them and when they are cultivated for the last time they are hilled up, and the weeds have been kept down, all without any hand work. At the last cultivation, kafir and milo are planted between the rows of potatoes and early garden stuff and there is plenty of time for it to mature and make fine large heads of grain for chicken feed.

Of all on her farm Mrs. Durnell is most interested in her flock of beautiful Rhode Island Reds. "I love them because they are so bright," she says, and they certainly seem to appreciate her kindness. Although they all look alike to a stranger, she knows every one by sight and calls them pet names as they feed from her hand. She knows which pullets lay the earliest and saves their eggs for hatching, for she has made a study of poultry as well as the other branches of farming, and knows that in this way she improves the laying qualities of the flock. "When starting my flock," said Mrs. Durnell, "I determined to have the best and I still get the best stock obtainable." She selects her breeders very carefully both for their early laying qualities and for their color and so has a flock of which any fancier might be proud as well as one that returns a good profit.

Everything is very carefully looked after on this little farm, nothing is wasted. The cleanings from the poultry house are spread over the garden because there are no grass or weed seeds mixed with them to become a nuisance. The cleanings from the cow barn are spread over the meadows and if there is grass seed among them so much the better for the meadow.

Nor has the inside of the house been neglected because

of the rush of work outside. Although this homemaker has learned to husband her strength and not do unnecessary things, still she has done the job thoroughly in the house also. Here are rare bits of old furniture brought from the old home, hand made, some of it, and hand carved. There is a fireplace, made according to Mrs. Durnell's own plan, with a chimney that draws even though she had to stand by the mason as he was building it and insist that he build it as she directed. There are pictures and bits of china and there are books and papers everywhere, the daily paper and the latest novel mingling in pleasant companionship with farm papers and bulletins.

Mrs. Durnell says she never has a dull moment, because farming is so interesting. And one can understand the reason why, after being with her in the house and going around with her over the farm.

The whole place is carefully planned for beauty, as well as profit. The house is set on a rise of ground which adds much to its appearance and at the same time will allow of the whole place being overlooked as it can all be seen from the front porch and windows. Just south of the house is the old spring, where marching bands of soldiers used to drink in war time.

Not far away is the sink hole, a place where the rock shell of the hills is crushed in, making a cup shaped hollow in the ground, which gathers the water from the surrounding hills when it rains. This water pours down through a crack in the rock, sometimes as large around as a barrel in volume, to flow through the crevices and caverns of the hills, emerging later, when purified by its journey; and flowing away in springs and creeks to join the waters of the Gasconade.

Mrs. Durnell has made a beautiful home out of a rough, wild piece of land and a wornout field and she now feels that it is established on a permanent paying basis. The fruits and garden with the cow and chickens more than furnish the living. The farm is growing in value every day, without any more very strenuous efforts on her part; and the home that she and Mr. Durnell planned for their old age is theirs, because of her determination and great good sense.

It has taken a great deal of hard work to accomplish this desired end, but it has been done without any worry. Mrs. Durnell early decided that the burden was heavy enough without adding to it a load of worry and so she chose as a motto for her life and work: "Just do your best and leave the rest"—and this she has lived up to through it all.

Her only regret is that she did not come to the farm when her children were small, for she says: "There is no place like a farm for raising children, where they can have in such abundance the fresh air and sunshine, with pure living water, good wholesome food and a happy outdoor life."

Laura explicitly drew on the farmer as pioneer analogy when she wrote the story of the Frinks and their Campriverside. Emma Frink, a gifted musician, was a close friend whom Laura knew through The Athenian Club in Hartville. With her husband, Mrs. Frink created a comfortable home and farm on the banks of the

Gasconade River called Campriverside. The Wilders were frequent visitors to Campriverside, and Missouri Ruralist *readers learned of its development in the June 1, 1921, issue. What this article highlights, as indeed do all of Laura's columns, is a deep and abiding love for the land and for the life of the farmer.*

PIONEERING ON AN OZARK FARM

The days of wilderness adventure are not past! The pioneer spirit is not dead!

We still have frontiers in our old, settled states where the joys of more primitive days may be experienced, with some of their hardships and now and then a touch of their grim humor.

Nestled in a bend of the Gasconade river $1\frac{3}{4}$ miles south of Hartville, the county seat of Wright County, is a little home which is gradually being made into a productive farm while losing none of its natural, woodland beauty. Its wild loveliness is being enhanced by the intelligent care it is receiving and the determination of its owners to take advantage of, and work with nature along the lines of her plans, instead of forcing her to change her ways and work according to man's ideas altogether—a happy co-operation with nature instead of a fight against her.

Mr. and Mrs. Frink, owners and partners in the farm, come of pioneer stock and never were quite content with town and village life. They often talked of the joys of pioneering and dreamed of going to the western frontiers somewhere.

Laura around 1917 when she was an active writer for the Missouri Ruralist.

And the years slipped by, leaving their imprint here and there a touch of snow in their dark hair; a few more lines around the eyes. Worst of all they found their health breaking. Mrs. Frink's nerves were giving way under the constant strain of teaching music and the combined efforts of each failed to pay the expenses of the many reverses, including doctor's bills with accompanying enforced idleness, and leave any surplus to be laid away for the old age that was bound to arrive with time.

All through the sweet days of spring and summer as Mrs. Frink sat hour after hour, working with some dull music pupil, she heard the call of the big outdoors and would forget to count the beat as she dreamed of pioneering in some wild, free place where, instead of hearing the false notes of beginners on the piano, she might listen to the music of the wild birds' song, the murmur of the wind among the tree tops and the rippling of some silver stream. And Mr. Frink fretted at the confinement of his law office and longed for wider spaces and the freedom of the old West he had known as a boy. But still they knew deep down in their hearts that there is no more frontier, in the old sense.

By chance, Mr. Frink found the little nook embraced by the bend of the river, tucked securely away in its hidden corner of the world and Mrs. Frink said, "This is our frontier, we will pioneer here!"

There were only 27 acres in the farm[—]mostly woodland, some flat, some set up edgeways and the rest at many different angles as is the way of land in the Ozarks, where, as has been said, we can farm three sides of the land thus getting the use of many more acres than our title deeds call for.

I think at no time did Mr. and Mrs. Frink see the farm as it actually was, but instead they saw it with the eye of faith as it should be later. What they bought were possibilities and the chance of working out their dreams. Mrs. Frink believed that here they could make their living and a little more. Mr. Frink was doubtful but eager to take a chance.

It required courage to make the venture for the place was in a bad state. There were some 6 or 7 acres of good bottom land in rather a poor state of cultivation and 7 acres of second bottom, or bench land, on which was an old thrown out, worn out field. The rest was woods land, a system of brush thickets a rabbit could hardly penetrate. The valleys and glens were overgrown with grape vines and poison ivy and abiding places of rattlesnakes and tarantulas. There were no fences worth the name.

The farm was bargained for in June, but negotiations were long and tedious for it was necessary to bring three persons to the same mind at the same time and it proved to be a case of many men of many minds instead. But at last the transaction was completed and one sunny morning in August, 1918, Mr. and Mrs. Frink gathered together their household goods and departed for the new home, on the frontier of the Ozarks, leaving Hartville without a mayor and its most prominent music teacher with one closed law and insurance office.

They went in a dilapidated hack, containing household goods and a tent, drawn by a borrowed horse. Hitched at the back of the hack was Mat, the Jersey cow, and Bessie Lee, her 9-month old calf. Dexter, a 4-month old colt, about 20 chickens and three shoats had been sent ahead with a lumber wagon.

At four o'clock that afternoon the tent was pitched at Campriverside and the Frinks were at home on their own farm. As Mr. Frink says, "The great problem was solved; we would not live our whole lives on a ½-acre lot."

For supper they feasted on roasting ears and ripe tomatoes from their own fields. These were principal articles of fare for some time. The green corn later gave place to "grits" and finally these were replaced by their own grown corn meal.

The Frinks began their life on the farm in a small way and handicapped by debt. The price of the land was $600, but after paying off old indebtedness there was left, of their capital, only $550 to pay for the land, build a house and buy a horse. For there was no house on the land and the tent must be the shelter until one could be built, while a horse was absolutely necessary to even a "one-horse farm."

Four hundred dollars was paid on the place and a note given for the balance of $200. Out of the remaining $150 a cabin was built and a horse bought. The material and labor in the house cost $120 and the horse cost $30.

Mr. and Mrs. Frink made up their minds at the start that the place must furnish fencing and building material as far as possible and really, log buildings seemed more in keeping with the rugged surroundings. The log house was built the first fall. It was 14 by 18 feet and a story and a half high. A shed for the stock, a chicken house and a good many rods of fence have been added since to the improvements.

From the first they lived from the proceeds of the little place. The land had been rented when bought and they were to have the owner's share from the 5 acres of corn on the bottom field. In the fall, the renter put 125 bushels of good, hard, white corn in the hastily constructed crib. The crop could have been cashed for $300.

The next fall there was 100 bushels of corn as their share from the rented field and a bunch of hogs raised on the place were sold for $125.

In 15 months after moving on the place the note for $200 and an old bill of $60 was paid off and a cream separator had been bought and paid for.

For the year of 1920 their share of corn was again 100 bushels, but because of the drop in prices only $70 worth of hogs were sold. The income from cream and eggs averaged a little over a dollar a day for 10 months of the year. And from the little new-seeded meadow, 2 tons of clover hay were cut and stacked.

The stock has been increased. There are now at home on the place, 3 good Jersey cows, a team of horses, 2 purebred Poland China brood sows, 10 shoats and 50 laying hens.

There is also on hand 600 pounds of dressed meat and stores of fruits and vegetables—the bulk of a year's provisions ahead. And best of all there are no debts but instead a comfortable bank account.

The expense of running the farm has been very little, about $25 a year for help. It is the intention that the eggs and cream shall provide money for running expenses, which so far they have done, leaving clear what money comes from selling the hogs, calves and surplus chickens.

The start in raising chickens was made under difficulties. Mrs. Frink was eager to begin stocking the place and early in the spring, when first the bargain was made for the farm, she

Though she left the farm for city life, Rose was nevertheless familiar with a poultry yard.

wished to raise some chickens to take to it. At that time the law forbade selling hens, so she borrowed one from a neighbor and set her. And that hen hatched out 11 roosters and only two pullets! Rather a discouraging start in the poultry business. But Mrs. Frink, while seeing the humor of the situation refused to admit failure. She took the 13 chickens out to the farm and put their coop up in a hickory tree beside the road. The roosters were fine, large Orpingtons and attracted the attention and admiration of the neighbors. Mrs. Frink refused to sell but offered to exchange for pullets and soon had a flock of 12 pullets and one rooster in the hickory tree. The pullets began laying in November, laid well all winter and raised a nice bunch of chicks in the spring.

The plans of these Ozark pioneers are not yet completed. Thirteen acres of the woodland are being cleared and seeded to timothy and clover. In the woods pasture the timber is being thinned, underbrush cleaned out and orchard grass, bluegrass and timothy is being sown.

Mr. Frink says, "There is much yet to be done. When the place is all cleared and in pasture it will support six cows, which means from $50 to $60 a month for cream and the fields in the bottom and on the bench will furnish grain for them and the hogs and chickens.

"We have demonstrated what can be done on a small piece of land even by renting out the fields. An ablebodied man could have done much better because he could have worked the fields himself and I would like to have more people know what a man with small means can accomplish."

Campriverside is located on the main fork of the Gasconade river, a section of country noted for its beautiful river and mountain scenery and Mrs. Frink's artist soul has found delight in the freedom and the beauties surrounding her. She says there is magic at Campriverside. An oak tree growing near the south side of the cabin, has the power, when atmospheric conditions are right, of seeming to talk and sing, being in some way a conductor of sounds of conversations and singing of neighbors living as far as a mile away. Among the branches of this tree, brushing the sides and roof of the house, birds of brilliant plumage and sweet song build their nests.

The rugged scenery and placid river had a greater charm for Mrs. Frink than the fertile soil of the bottom land and she took time each day to explore her little kingdom. Many were the beauty spots she discovered.

There were the basins in the rocks below the spring and Pulpit Rock which she desecrated by setting her tub upon it when she washed.

When the spring rises and makes a brook in the little glen, there are the Cascades and Wildcat Falls.

And there is Wild Cat Den where at rare intervals the bobcat screams, calling the mate who has been the victim of encroaching civilization, while just below is Fern Glen where magnificent sword ferns grow.

As if these were not enough natural beauties for one small farm, there are the Castle Rocks and the Grotto and the dens where the woodchucks and minks live.

And there are wild flowers everywhere—"wild flowers that mark the footsteps of the Master as He walks in His garden and the brilliant coloring of the autumn foliage speaks again of His presence."

Through the Ruralist *years, Laura occasionally wrote of early pioneer days, basing her articles on her own experiences, and occasionally on those of others she met. "When Grandma Pioneered" appeared in the August 1, 1921, issue of the* Ruralist. *Unfortunately, the Grandma referred to in the article was unnamed and has never been identified. It is clear from the article, though, how much Laura esteemed the hard work and courage of the early generation in their efforts to carve out a life for themselves and their families in the wilderness.*

WHEN GRANDMA PIONEERED

Grandma was minding the baby—. "Oh, yes, she is sweet," she said, "but she is no rarity to me. You see there were ten of us at home and I was the oldest save one and that a boy. Seems like I've always had a baby to take care of. There were the little ones at home then when I was older I used to go help the neighbors at times and there was always a new baby, for women them days didn't hire help unless they were down sick. When I was married I had 11 of my own; now it's the grandchildren—No indeed! Babies are no rarity to me! I was just a child myself when father and mother drove an ox team into the Ozarks. Father stopped the wagon in the thick woods by the big road; cut down some trees and made a rough log cabin. But mother never liked the house there; father was away so much and she didn't like to stay alone with the young ones so near the road. The Ozarks was a wild, rough country then and all kinds of persons were passing, so father built another house down by the spring out of sight and we lived there.

"The woods were full of wild turkeys and deer; when we children hunted the cows at night we thought nothing of seeing droves of them. Snakes were thick, too, and not so pleasant to meet, but none of us ever got bit tho we went barefoot all summer and until freezing weather.

"Father used to tan the hides of deer and cattle and make our shoes but later we had 'boughten' shoes. Then the men of the settlement would drive their ox teams south into the pineries in the fall and haul in logs to the mills. When they had hauled a certain number of loads they were paid with a load of logs for themselves. These they had sawed into lumber and hauled the lumber to Springfield or Marshfield 75 or 100 miles, and sold it to get their tax money and shoes for the family.

"The men worked away a good deal and the mothers and children made the crops. Neighbors were few and far apart but we were never lonely, didn't have time to be. We raised wheat and corn for our bread; hogs ran loose in the woods and with venison and wild turkey made our meat; we kept some sheep for the wool and we raised cotton.

"After we had gathered the cotton from the fields we hand picked it from the seeds. We carded the cotton and wool and then spun them into yarn and thread and wove them into cloth; we made our own blankets and coverlets and all the cloth we used, even our dresses.

"We worked long days. As soon as we could see, in the morning, two of us would go into the woods and drive up the oxen for the days work. Then we girls worked all day in the fields while mother worked both in the house and out. Soon as supper was over we built a brush fire in the fireplace to make light and while one tended the fire to keep it bright the others spun and wove and knit and sewed until 10 and 11 o'clock. Passing a house after dark, any time before midnight you could always hear the wheel a whirring and the loom at work. We cooked in the fireplace too, and I was 16 years old before I ever saw a cook stove.

"When the crops were raised, mother and we children did the threshing. The wheat was spread on poles with an old blanket under them to catch the grain as it dropped thru and we bailed it out with hickory poles, then blew the dust out in the wind and it was ready to take to mill.

"We were taught to be saving. The shoes bought in the fall must last a year and we were careful with them. When they got calico into the country it cost 25 cents a yard and if we had a calico dress we wore it for very best. When we took it off we brushed off all the dust, turned it, folded it and laid it carefully away.

"I never got much schooling. There was three months school in the year beginning the first Monday in September but that was molasses making, potato digging, corn picking time and we older children had to stay home and do the work. The little ones went and by the time they were older we had things in better shape so they got lots more learning. But it was too late for us.

"Now school comes before the work at home and when children go to school it takes all their time; they can't do anything else.

"I wish folks now had to live for a little while like we did when I was young, so they would know what work is and learn to appreciate what they have. They have so much they are spoiled, yet every cent they get they must spend for something more. They want cars and pianos and silk dresses— Why when I was married all my wedding clothes were of my own spinning and weaving, but my husband was so proud he wouldn't let me wear my linsey dresses but bought me calico instead.

"Ah well, times have changed! I'm an old woman and have worked hard all my life but even now I can work down some of the young ones."

MRS. WILDER'S NATURE SONGS

Nature—its beauties, moods, and teachings—inspired Laura's earliest writing on the prairies of Dakota Territory. The abundant natural surroundings of her Rocky Ridge Farm in the foothills of the Ozarks also inspired her to write, just as the prairie landscape had. While Laura wrote for the Missouri Ruralist, *she was able to publish some of her nature poetry within its pages. In this way, "Mrs. Wilder's Nature Songs" found their way into print when space was available in the* Ruralist. *Most of Laura's poems were simply written for her own pleasure, and, as she said, "Just to relieve my feeling."*

The Song of the Autumn Breeze

The Autumn breeze sang a tender song,
And our noses were blue and our faces long:
And the time and the tune, both seemed all wrong,
For winter had come too soon.

Oh, "The Autumn breeze sang a tender song:"
And our fuel was short, and our store bill long;
While taxes and troubles came in a throng:
And winter had only begun.

"The Autumn breeze sang a tender song,"
Of an overcoat, that was worn too long:

Of last year's clothes and our pride so strong:
And our summer wages gone.

We hear a tale when the breezes sing
Of the easy money we made last spring
Of how that money has taken wing
Oh, the Autumn breeze sings a *tender* song.

The Wilders discovered that Ozark winters, unlike the Dakota ones, gave way early to springtime. By late February or March, Almanzo was busy plowing the garden plot, and the first blooming wildflowers and blossoms made the hills look like a huge garden. Spring made Laura eager to plant the crops and garden again, and watch for the changing landscape to be transformed from dormancy to life. She commemorates the season in this poem.

Springtime on Rocky Ridge

The wild woods things are calling
And the heart in answer thrills,
For it's spring time in the Ozarks
It is bloom time in the Hills.
The dogwood blooms along the "draws"
The redbud's all aglow
The pears and plums and cherries
Look like wreaths of drifted snow
The buttercups and violets
Have blossomed over night

The peach trees all are showing pink
And the apple trees are white.

Had the Wilders been born a few generations later, they might well have been environmentalists and staunch participants of the back-to-nature movement. Although they spent years developing their house on Rocky Ridge Farm, they took equal pride and interest in the hills, meadows, forests, and ravines of their land. Their recreational activities included walking, horseback riding, picnicking, and exploring in the countryside. Laura's love of her Ozark homeland is evident in this verse.

Come to the Woods with Me
Did you ever ride down a bridle path
'Neath tall old moss grown trees,
Reins lying loose on the horse's neck,
Cheek fanned by the soft cool breeze?

Did you ever drink from a flowing spring
Deep in the heart of the wood,
While grim old trees like sentinels,
Around the place have stood?

Did you ever lie in the cooling shade
And listen to squirrel and bird
Chatting away in their woodland speech,
When they didn't know they were heard?

Laura swinging on an Ozark grapevine on Rocky Ridge Farm.

Or ever notice the hush that falls,
On all the forest talk,
When high in the sky above is heard
The wild fierce cry of the hawk?

Did you ever stand in a lonely spot,
'Neath the mountains' deep'ning frown
And watch the gathering shadows creep,
After the sun goes down?

These are the joys of a life in the woods,
Where every breath is sweet,
The shades are soft and you hear the noise
Of little scurrying feet.

When your brain is tired and heart is sore,
With the longing to be free,
Then turn away from the crowds of men
And come to the woods with me.

Although the Wilders spent most of their adult lives in the Ozarks, they never quite lost a feeling of nostalgia for the prairies of South Dakota. Whether it was a longing for the place of their youth or for their first years together as a married couple, Laura could not say. But in her most lengthy poem, Laura explores her love for the prairies throughout the seasons.

Spring
Like a gigantic meadow, spreads the prairie wide and
   green
And here and there the violets, add a purple sheen.
The air is fresh and balmy and little breezes sing,
In the Spring.

In the hush of early morn, when the dew is on the grass,
And bright hued clouds go sailing by, as night-time
   shadows pass,

The world is full of music, for the Meadow larks sing,
In the Spring.

Summer
Oh it's Summer time
And roses, come together,
On the Prairie.
The Prairie Rose!
The Prairie Rose!
We'll sing its praises ever.
Oh it's Summer time
And June time
And Bloom time
All together,
For Summer time and rose time
Come together
On the Prairie.
Oh it's long bright days,
Of sunshine, on the Prairies.
In the Summer.
Oh Prairies green,
Or Prairies brown,
Our love for you ne'er wearies.
Because of sunshine
And moonshine
And starshine
And the Prairies,

Laura and Almanzo (left) picnicking with friends at Williams Cave.

The days and nights are perfect,
On the Prairies.

Autumn

Ever I see them, with my memory's vision,
As first my eyes beheld them, years agone,
Clad all in brown, with russet shades and golden,
Stretching away into the far unknown.

Never a break to mar their sweep of grandeur,
From North to South, from East to West, the same,

Save that the East was full of purple shadows,
The West, with setting sun, was all aflame.

Never a sign of human habitation,
To show that man's dominion was begun,
The only marks, the footpaths of the Bison,
Made by the herds, before their day was done.

The sky downturned, a brazen bowl above me;
And clanging with the calls of wild gray geese,
Winging their way into the distant South-land;
To 'scape the coming storms and rest in peace.

Ever the winds went whispering o'er the prairie,
Ever the grasses whispered back again;
And then the sun dipped down below the sky-line;
And stars lit just the outlines of the plain.

Winter

Who can describe a Winter, of the North, upon the
     plains?
How tell the fury of the winds, when the Storm King
     reigns?
How sing the song of a whirling world of snow,
Or catch the rhythmetic measure that the storm winds
     blow?
There is fury incarnate, in their attack so bold.

There is might, in their sweep and the fierceness of their
   cold.
They are cruel as death and as fate are strong,
With the wild music of the Sagas in their song.

On the still, cold nights, of Winter,
When the Heavens seem so low,
That one can almost touch the stars,
From the world of drifted snow;
The psalmist's song comes ringing down,
From the ages long ago.

"The heavens declare the Glory of God; and the firmament
   showeth His handiwork.
Day unto day uttereth speech and night unto night showeth
   knowledge.
There is no speech nor language where their voice is not
   heard.
Their line is gone out through all the earth and their words to
   the end of the world."

You ask me to sing you a song of the plains,
Of the wide treeless wastes where the free winds blow.
Shall I sing of their beauties when green in the Spring,
or tell of their terrors when swept by the snow?

Shall I tell of their cold, their heat and their storms,
Of their warm, bright days and their dusty weather,

Of how they are loved and are hated at once,
For their kindness and cruelty blended together?

Oh yes! I will sing you a song of the plains.
I love them and hate them and fear them, but still,
I will sing you a song of their beauty and charm,
The while I rest safe in the lee of a hill.

LAURA AND HER HOMETOWN

Community life was thriving in America around the turn of the century. The first difficulties of pioneering had been overcome, and small towns like Mansfield, Missouri, were bustling centers of trade. Community pride and spirit were strong; each town liked to boast about its school, band, baseball team, and public buildings.

When the Wilder family moved to the town of Mansfield, during the lean years when they were waiting for their Rocky Ridge Farm apple orchard to bear fruit, Laura and Almanzo wholeheartedly entered into the social and civic life of the town. They could hardly stay aloof from what was going on; their house in Mansfield stood on the main road that led east out of town, toward Rocky Ridge Farm. In their years in town, from 1898 to 1910, Almanzo became Mansfield's drayman, and Laura cooked and served meals to travelers and railroad workers. Laura also became active in local politics and served in the Mansfield National Farm Loan Association.

Involved as they became in the town community, it was natural for Laura to look at activities and situations around her as possible writing topics. She knew what local color was, and she realized that Mansfield offered plenty of good stories that might interest folks who lived outside the Ozarks. When she began to publish such stories in Kansas City and St. Louis newspapers, her friends and neighbors took notice.

The pioneer girl who loved the lonely prairie became a well-known citizen of her new hometown of Mansfield. People thought

On August 24, 1908, Mansfield turned out to watch Ava Quigley drive the golden spike that officially started construction of a spur linking the Kansas City, Ozark, and Ava Southern Railway from Mansfield to Ava. Laura, wearing elbow-length black gloves, is second from the left of Ava.

well of Laura. Her community regarded her as a real asset to the town because of her creativity, business sense, and good-natured friendliness. She was a spokesperson for townspeople and farmers alike—so much so that she was even encouraged to make a bid for public office! These articles, first published in a variety of newspapers, show Laura's keen eye for detail and ability to capture personalities. They also show her great interest in all aspects of her community, from political to religious to social.

The debate over a jail for the town of Mansfield gave Laura material for a feature story published in the St. Louis Globe-Democrat *on May 8, 1916. Her use of the names Tom, Dick, and Harry were obviously an easy method of obscuring the identities of specific individuals—maybe neighbors—who might object to being written about in print.*

MANSFIELD GETS A JAIL

"What's our jail fur, I'd like to know," said Tom. "Fur an or-na-mint, I reckon," replied Dick. "Hit shore hain't needed fur nawthing but to look purty," added Harry.

The town marshall, of Mansfield, Missouri, had just started for Hartville, with a prisoner. He was such an important prisoner that the County Jail at Hartville was the only proper place for him.

Excitement had died down somewhat and Tom, Dick and Harry sat on the steps in front of Reynolds' store, discussing the arrest with its attendant circumstances.

Mansfield had been forging to the front, of late, with a Young Men's Business Club, a moving picture theater and the "good roads" movement, but there are still a few conservative citizens who love to gather in quiet places on the walks and exchange private opinions on public questions.

"Hit's come to a purty pass," said Uncle Joe, "when a feller hain't allowed to speak to a man just because he's arrested."

"Speak to him," exclaimed Uncle Simon. "The boy warn't allowed to come nigh him; and just because he wouldn't be driv away like a dog they arrested the boy and fined him."

"The boys don't git a fair show in this town no more no how," said Uncle Rube. "What kin they do fur a time with the dogs taxed till a feller can't keep more'n five or six and a jail sentence staring him in the face if they take a leetle too much. We got along well enough when we hadn't a jail."

The story of how Mansfield came to be without a jail goes back to the time when there was a calaboose of sorts down by Hoover's mule barn. This structure was 12 × 14 and a scant one story high. The door was of oak slabs fastened with iron hasps and a padlock. There were no windows. Why should there be? Was it not the intention to place criminals "in durance vile", and anyway the door was opened once in a while.

The last prisoner to occupy this stronghold was incarcerated as the direct result of the preceding city election. The breath of reform had put a new tang in the Ozark breezes and the town had gone "dry", also the constable elected on the reform ticket had made pre-election promises to arrest every "drunk and disorderly" he found within the city limits.

The stand-patters for the old order of things said, "He'd be so durned anxious to arrest somebody that it wouldn't be safe to whittle the adge of the board walk no more."

This suggestion came near to defeating the reform ticket, for no free and independent citizen would stand for having his rights taken from him in this manner.

The reform candidate had to promise that he would not interfere with the established custom. For the board walk, which reached from the schoolhouse on the east, through the residence part of town, past the business houses on the square and through the residence district on the other side clear to McNaul's addition on the west, fulfilled all the uses of a club, warm in the sun in winter, cool in the shade in summer, a place where a fellow could sit comfortably on the high places with his feet hanging off, whittle the edge of the boards and talk politics or the latest scandle.

But though the board walk must be left undisturbed, the new constable could show his zeal for cleaning up the town by arresting a hobo. This would surely be playing safe for there could be no question of a come-back at the next election, so what might have been overlooked in one of "the boys" could not, would not be neglected in this stranger in the midst. It was a chance to make good.

This hobo, in a somewhat befuddled condition, insisted on preaching, taking his stand on the railroad crossing near the square.

The result was that he was landed in the calaboose at the hands of the zealous, new, reform constable. There he was left to meditate, and the constable went comfortably home to dinner, knowing that his prisoner would await his return, being secured by hasps and padlock.

Along in the afternoon one of the loafers on the board walk stopped his whittling on the edge thereof to gaze inquiringly over toward Hoover's mule barn.

"What do you reckon that smoke is over there Jake?" he drawled. All the crowd on the board walk, within hearing, gazed in the direction indicated, and Jake rose suddenly to his feet.

"Come on boys," he said. "Some durn fool has dropped a match in Hoover's mule barn and set the dummed thing afire." It was not the mule barn however. It was the humble jail that nestled in its shelter.

Smoke was pouring out of the cracks around the door of the Jail and rising from a hole burned in the roof. As the "boys" came nearer they could hear a frenzied pounding on the door and muffled cries. Nearer still, they could distinguish the voice of the hobo in frantic prayer. "Oh, Lord," he cried. "I know I am an awful sinner, but save me this time, and I'll never touch another drop." As he heard the men at the door a stream of curses poured forth, enough to set the rest of the building in a blaze ending up with, "why don't you blankety, blank, blank fools let me out of here? If you don't, when I do get out I'll tear your hearts out."

The constable was not there, nor the key. They tried to pull the lock off, to an accompaniment of curses from the prisoner, prone on the floor with his mouth to the crack at the bottom of the door, the only place where the breathing was good. As the lock stayed fast, the men scattered, one to find the constable, others to give the alarm. One alone stayed, and as the voices of the others died away and the noise of their going ceased, the voice of the hobo in frantic prayer came through the crack at the bottom of the door.

"Oh, Lord, save me and I'll never get drunk again! Oh, Lord, let me out and I'll never touch another drop."

The man on the outside waited a moment then stepped over to the barn and came back with an axe. At the first noise of his movements the tone of the voice beneath the door changed. A volley of curses came out ending with, "You blanked fool, let me out of here or I'll burn down your blanked jail."

The jail door was battered down just as the crowd from downtown came rushing up. In the excitement the hobo slipped away and the last seen of him he was beating it down the railroad track as fast as he could count the ties. He paused on the horizon line, pulled a bottle from his pocket, raised it to his lips for a long moment, then dropped it on the ground and disappeared into Rock Cut. He had not paused for explanations, but it had been gathered from his conversation before his exit that he had set his downy couch of straw on fire to burn his way to freedom, forgetting that the inside of his prison would be sure to burn first.

Thus Mansfield was without a jail, but it was unnecessary, anyway. Tramps could be run out of town, and when any of "the boys" got "into trouble" they could leave town for a few days or weeks according to the seriousness of the "trouble" and come back when it had blown over, without making the city any expense: then to be sure there was always the County Jail at Hartville.

This plan was not always satisfactory however, for instance, the time when Mansfield first passed the stock law and undertook to put all stray animals in the pound.

When some cattle belonging to a near-by farmer strayed into town and were put in the livery yard used for a pound, the farmer shouldered his shotgun, walked into town, opened the yard gate and drove his cattle home, the shotgun on his shoulder speaking so eloquently that no other speech was necessary.

Later he allowed himself to be arrested and taken to Hartville Jail, where, to save expense and trouble, he being a good fellow, the Sheriff allowed him to serve his ten days' sentence visiting around among his kin folks.

This would never do for how could the majesty of the law be upheld with "sich goings on?" So it began to be talked along the board walk that Mansfield needed a jail.

You must know that when anything was talked along the board walk, it was a long talk, for the walk reached, you remember, from the schoolhouse hill down through town, on Commercial Avenue, past the square and clear out to McNaul's addition.

It began to be talked, as I said, along the board walk that Mansfield must have a jail, but the talk was without much effect until something serious happened and a place of detention was badly needed.

A murderer came to town! The marshall knew him at once from the description of him which had been sent out, so when the marshall saw him slinking around waiting for a chance to hop a train he started for him. The outlaw was quick to take the hint and a running chase started through the street that would have done credit to a movie film. Every man and boy in sight joined in and finally—the murderer escaped in the woods. But just suppose they had caught him, what would they have done with him? It was nearly night and who would have taken the long ride to Hartville, through the woods in the darkness of night with a desperate murderer?

It was decided, from one end of the board walk to the other, that Mansfield must have a jail. The questions were how, when, where and what of. These queries kept the board walk buzzing for some time.

There must be an increase in the city tax for the how.

"We're taxed enough now," growles Bill, as he whittles one corner of the board walk. He did not think a jail was needed. The "boys" could always leave town at a moment's notice.

"Better put a tax on dogs," answered Hi. "A dollar a piece on them fourteen hounds of yourn would help some."

It was a clear case of personal animosity on his part because Bill had one more hound then Hi had.

"Hit stands to reason," said Uncle Bob, "that we don't need no jail. Hit'll only burn up again 'nd Dave won't have it down by his mule barn no more. Say's hit's too dangerous. Might have burned up his mules."

"I'll tell you," said Ben who had a saw mill. "Build her of oak planks. They won't burn easy, anyway while they're green."

"Huh!" spoke up Sam who owned the brick yard.

"They'd burn when they dried. Build it of brick."

"Yes," said Jim who sold cement at the lumber yard, "and have your dad-gummed brick fall to pieces in the first rain. What we want is a jail built of concrete. It won't burn nor melt in the rain and the feller don't live can break out of it if it's built right," and as Jim was popular and a leader in the lodge, he had his way in the end.

For greater strength the jail was built in the form of a half-cylinder and all of one piece like a jug. It was built on a piece of ground that would never, could never be used for any better purpose, it was so straight up and down. Being just over the hill to the south of town, it is nearly or quite out of sight, so that Mansfield has the appearance of still being without a jail, especially as the building when seen would never be identified.

The Mansfield Jail in the early 1900's.

This jail has been used with judgment. The first time one of "the boys" had a drop too much of spring-water—Mansfield is still dry—and became a little unruly, he was put in the new jail just as dark was coming on and the marshall went away, purposely leaving the door wide open. When the prisoner with his befuddled mind found the open door and got out, he thought he had broken jail and went home to stay in hiding for a day or two. After that the jail was rented to store dynamite in for use in building the Kansas City and Ozarks Southern Railroad.

All these things were known to Tom, Dick and Harry as they sat on the stone coping in front of Reynolds' store, with others of the old guard and discussed town affairs.

"Yes, Mansfield's got a jail," said Uncle Ben, "but what's hit good fur? Just to pay taxes fur and to help build this durn new railroad that's jest a damage to the kentry. Hits put every freighter out of business between Mansfield and Ava."

"Speaking of taxes," exclaimed Uncle Jeff, "see how they soaked us to pay fur thet new schoolhouse up thar on the hill. Fifteen hundred dollars fur a house fur young 'uns to go to school in."

"They dew say," said Uncle Rube, "that there's a room in the basement fur the 'children to exercise in'. We used to git exercise enough in the corn patch, but they say they are teaching them ag-ri-culture at the school now."

When the Wilders first arrived in Mansfield, Missouri, in 1894, they discovered that their accustomed denomination, the

Congregational Church, was not established in town. So they became affiliated with the Methodist Church instead, and were loyal churchgoers there until they died. When a church history was being prepared in the 1950's, Laura was interviewed about the origins of Methodism in Mansfield. She told of the dedication of the white frame church in 1900, with an indebtedness of only $15. As if mourning a lost pleasure, she recalled the huge tins of gingerbread and slabs of biscuits she had baked for church suppers and socials.

As is common in many towns, churches sometimes shared ministers and combined their organizations, with parishioners visiting back and forth. The Wilders sometimes attended revivals and "singings" at other churches in the area. Laura's description of the Prairie Hollow Church south of Mansfield commemorates a Baptist-ritual Sunday.

SACRAMENT SUNDAY AT PRAIRIE HOLLOW CHURCH

The second Sunday of May is the day of the yearly sacrament at Prairie Hollow Church, when the members of this General Baptist Church eat the Blessed Bread and drink the wine and perform the sacred ceremony of foot washing, a custom of the primitive church which is becoming obsolete.

Prairie Hollow Church was built in a little hollow of the hills whose timbered heights enclose it. The grass grows green and sweet around up to the worn stone steps at the very door and the dead who have belonged to this congregation sleep peacefully in the adjoining cemetery where the white headstones show among the wild flowers, where the wild birds sing and the wind in the tree tops whispers softly. And they seemed not quite so lonely being at rest so near the church, within sound of the singing of their old friends who gather near them so often.

Early, while the morning freshness still lay over the hills and dew drops glistened in shady places the people began to gather. They came in wagons, in buggies, on horseback, in motor cars and on foot. The cars were parked near by, horses and mules tied to wagons and trees, while the people went into the "churchhouse" for the song service. The morning was dedicated to Mother, it being Mother's Day, and it was curious and in a way refreshing to step back into a day that is past and hear from the pulpit that "woman's place is in the home, raising and training the children," that women should do this because "they are responsible for saving the world, having brought sin into the world."

By the way, although it is not compulsory, women and girls still sit on the right side of the church while the men and boys gather on the left in the good old fashioned way.

When noon came tablecloths were spread on the clean grass at one side of the church and the women emptied their laden baskets upon them. The well cooked meats, light, nutty flavored breads, delicious pies, cakes, canned fruit, pickles and salads, the abundance and variety, the fact that the food prepared by this large crowd of country women was all good shows that the cooking departments in country schools are superfluous. In this "neck of the woods" at least, mothers can still teach their daughters to cook.

The friendliness, the fellowship, the hospitality shown by the crowd would have been a revelation to one not accustomed to such a dinner. There was not room enough to sit at the cloth so after Grace had been said each one helped himself to what he wanted, drawing back to make room for others to do the same. We ate standing, moving around from group to group, praising the food and the cooks, helping each other to desired portions. There was no crowding, no rudeness, nothing to offend fastidiousness.

After the hour of eating and visiting came another song service in the church and then the sermon, the sacrament including the foot washing. It is a quaint custom and made solemn and beautiful by the spirit which enters into it—the spirit of humility and willingness to serve others which is so

Mansfield's Commercial Street, looking west. The town square, the center of community life, is seen at left.

visibly expressed by the lowly and menial task of washing each other's feet. As the preacher stooped to be the first to humble himself he said "I am willing to be your servant for a servant is not greater than his Lord." And this was the keynote of the sermon "serve one another for the need of mankind is service, service for each other, service for humanity."

Looking around me at the earnest faces while this great need was emphasized, listening to the singing of the old hymns "If I may drink of the fount of love, I'll be satisfied then" and "Lord plant my feet on higher ground," the earnestness, the devoutness of this congregation of hard working people put a hope in my heart that in spite of the confusion and contention abroad on earth, "God is still in His Heaven" and all will be "right with the world."

In her forum within the pages of the Missouri Ruralist, *Laura discussed everything from household tips to manners, and from house building to the raising of children. Eventually, her thoughts turned to women's issues. She had commented during her courtship with Almanzo that she saw no need for women to vote, but over time her opinion came to change. When women were first allowed to vote in 1918, Laura was delighted. She attempted to encourage her fellow townswomen to cast their first ballots, and wrote about the exciting development as well. In the December 5, 1919, issue of the* Missouri Ruralist, *she aired her views on politics and a woman's place in public life.*

A Few Words to Voters

Is one any more of a lawbreaker, I wonder, for trying to take that to which he is not entitled from those above him in the social scale, than for taking more than he is entitled to from those below him in the social scale?

Some public speakers and some editorials are saying that the farmers hold the balance of power and will have to take control and handle the situation. But farmers are only partly organized, and it will be difficult for them to handle anything so few understand; besides, they are all divided among political parties and stand by their particular party regardless, even though by so doing they lower prices.

I heard some farmers talking politics not long ago, and they violently disagreed, passing insults on one another's popular leaders. In this they were following the lead of their daily papers.

Some writers are expressing the hope that the women will "clean house" in politics, sweeping out from both parties those who only clutter up the place and hinder the day's work.

I think the idea of a woman's party, a political division on sex lines, is distasteful to women, especially farm women. It seems as if the time has come to reason together instead of dividing into another antagonistic group.

If women, with their entrance into a free discussion of politics, can do away with the "hot air" and insults, with "making the Eagle scream," and "twisting the Lion's tail," and "shaking the bloody shirt," and all the rest of the smoke screen, bringing politics into the open air of sane, sensible discussion, a discussion of facts and conditions, not personal discussions of leaders, they will have rendered the country a great service.

Local politics were among Laura's main activities during 1919. A loyal Democrat like her husband, Laura helped to get other local women interested in political candidates. That summer a group of women from a Democratic organization from Pleasant Valley Township (the area where Rocky Ridge Farm was located) met at The Bank of Mansfield and elected Laura chair of the Wright County Democratic Committee. In this capacity, Laura attended similar meetings at the county seat of Hartville and as far away as Rolla.

The following year, Laura published an editorial in the Missouri Ruralist *supporting the administration of Governor Frederick Gardner, and she received an official letter of appreciation from the state capital at Jefferson City. Laura also enthusiastically supported N. J. Craig of Mansfield in his bid for prosecuting attorney. She wrote to a possible supporter:*

I do not know what your politics are but I . . . ask you to vote for Mr. N. J. Craig for prosecuting attorney if you can possibly do so. Mr. Craig has been a great help to us in our Farm Loan Association. There is no doubt that without his help we would not have had the Association and so I think we ought to show our appreciation by giving him our votes. Mr. Craig will make a good prosecuting attorney. We know this from his past record and his reputation. If you

Greetings From Mansfield, Mo.　　In The Beautiful Ozark Country

Postcard of Mansfield in the 1940's, as the Wilders knew it.

are a Democrat I'm sure you will vote for him and if you are a Republican I hope you will put his name on your ticket.

Five years later, in the spring of 1925, Laura herself sought political office, as Collector for Pleasant Valley Township. Her earlier work as Secretary Treasurer for the Mansfield National Farm Loan Association qualified her for this job, and she looked upon the salary of $300 per year as a good supplement to the farm income. The Mansfield Mirror *published Laura's campaign statement to the local voters.*

I have been asked to place my name before the voters of Pleasant Valley Township, as candidate for the office of

Collector in the election of March 31, 1925.

Mr. Wilder and I came to Wright county thirty years ago, and bought the farm east of Mansfield where we now live. My character is known to neighbors and friends throughout the county. I have been a busy farm woman and have not had time to do as much for the community as I would have liked to do, but wherever possible I have done my best.

Seven years ago, with eight other farmers, I organized the Mansfield National Farm Loan Association, which I have served ever since as Secretary Treasurer. The Association now has 54 members. As its Secretary Treasurer I have been entrusted with $102,675 United States Government money, which the Association has loaned to farmers in this community at 5½ per cent interest. I believe that this amount of money, brought into our community from the government has increased our prosperity by that much, and has been of direct or indirect value to us all.

I have personally handled all the details of these loans and been responsible for the money. Federal Bank Examiners certify that I have attended promptly to the business and that my records are always accurate and in order. I believe the members of the Farm Loan Association who receive an 8 percent dividend on their stock every year, will testify that my work has been satisfactory to them.

After these seven years of experience, I am confident that I can perform the duties of Collector of Pleasant Valley Township accurately, and to the satisfaction of the tax payers.

I am not a politician and have no thought of entering politics, but I appreciate very much the compliment of being asked to be a candidate for this office, and if elected I shall serve the tax payers of the Township as faithfully as I have served the Farm Loan Association, the Farm Club and other community organizations with which I have been connected, I shall of course have an office in Mansfield and I shall attend to all business promptly and carefully.

On Election Day, March 31, 1925, Laura was soundly beaten. Rose suspected some questionable vote-counting and ad-mitted she was disappointed. "But thank goodness, Mama Bess* doesn't awfully mind," she wrote to an inquiring friend.

Never again did Laura run for a public office, but she remained keenly interested in both politics and government for the rest of her life.

Mansfield, like most small American towns, organized groups for culture and study. These study clubs, often limited in member-ship and sometimes quite exclusive, formed the backbone of adult education in the community. Laura eagerly joined each club as it was formed, and she was readily accepted as an active member. While the clubs were very social, they were also precise in their goals, rules, and customs.

Laura's long association with The Athenians began when the club was formed in February 1916, at the county seat of Hartville, eleven miles north of Mansfield. "He who profits most serves best"

---

* Laura's middle name was Elizabeth, and so Rose nicknamed her mother Mama Bess. Almanzo called Laura Bessie.

Laura Ingalls Wilder Day at the Wright County Library on August 2, 1950, was sponsored by The Athenians. Laura, seated, is greeting Mary Day; at right are two other friends, Emma Frink and Melissa Wilson.

was the club motto, and the original goal of the members was to establish a library and a community room specifically for women. The onetime initiation fee of $25 was donated to further these projects. Each of the twenty Athenians was expected to entertain in turn when the club met on the third Wednesday of the month. Subject matter varied; in 1919 the members studied various authors and reported on writings of Shakespeare, Dickens, Hawthorne, Mark Twain, and others. In 1921, topics members studied included "Late Inventions and Discoveries," "Interstate Church Movement," "Prominent People," and "Interesting Places." Laura herself presented the topic "State Officers and Their Duties."

Laura's association with The Athenians was lifelong; her

name was still on the roster of membership at the time of her death. Through the years, the club was proud and honored to follow Laura's flourishing writing career, and periodically she was asked to update the group on her books and their progress. Laura was modest in discussing herself, almost apologetic when she referred to the books she wrote. In August of 1950, The Athenians sponsored a Laura Ingalls Wilder Day at the Wright County Library in Hartville. Laura attended, signed autographs, and shook hands with lines of people who came to honor her.

Soon after Laura joined The Athenians, she wrote about the organization in a column titled "Folks Are 'Just Folks'" in the May 5, 1916, issue of the Missouri Ruralist. *Her democratic nature and disdain for the snobbery that separated town dwellers and country farmers is alluded to in this essay, which is subtitled "Why Shouldn't Town and Country Women Work and Play Together?" Laura was, significantly, one of the few farm women who participated in The Athenians.*

Folks Are "Just Folks"

"The Athenians" is a woman's club just lately organized, in Hartville, for purposes of study and self-improvement. Hartville was already well supplied with social organizations. There was an embroidery club, also a whist club, and the usual church aid societies and secret orders which could do so much in country towns. Still there were a few busy women who felt something lacking. They could not be satisfied altogether with social affairs. They wanted to cultivate their minds and increase their knowledge, so they organized the little study club and have laid out a year's course of study.

The membership of the club is limited to twenty. If one of the twenty drops out then some one may be elected to take the vacant place. Two negative ballots exclude anyone from membership. There are no dues. "The Athenians" is, I think, a little unique for a town club, as the membership is open to town and country women alike and there are several country members. Well, why not? "The Colonel's lady and Judy O'Grady are sisters under the skin." (Mind I have not said whether Judy O'Grady is a town or country woman. She is just as likely, if not a little more likely, to be found in one place as the other.)

Surely the most vital subjects in which women are interested are the same in town and country, while the treasures of literature and the accumulated knowledge of the world are for all alike. Then why not study them together and learn to know each other better? Getting acquainted with folks makes things pleasanter all around. How can we like people if we do not know them? It does us good to be with people whose occupation and surroundings are different from ours. If their opinions differ from ours, it will broaden our minds to get their point of view and we will likely find that they are right in part at least, while it may be that a mutual understanding will lead to a modification of both opinions.

While busily at work one afternoon I heard the purr of a motor and going to the door to investigate, I was met by the smiling faces of Mr. and Mrs. Frink and Mr. and Mrs. Curtis of Hartville. Mrs. Curtis and Mrs. Frink have taken an active part in organizing "The Athenians" and they had come over to tell me of my election to membership in that club. What should be done when there is unexpected company and one is totally unprepared and besides must be at once hostess, cook and maid? The situation is always so easily handled in a story. The lovely hostess can perform all kinds of conjuring tricks with a cold bone and a bit of left over vegetable, producing a delicious repast with no trouble whatever and never a smut on her beautiful gown. In real life it sometimes is different, and during the first of that pleasant afternoon my thoughts would stray to the cook's duties. When the time came, however, it was very simple. While I made some biscuit, Mrs. Frink fried some home cured ham and fresh eggs, Mrs. Curtis set the table. The-Man-Of-The-Place opened a jar of preserves and we all had a jolly, country supper together before the Hartville people started on the drive home. It is such a pleasure to have many friends and to have them dropping in at unexpected times that I have decided when it lies between friendships and feasting and something must be crowded out the feasting may go every time.

At a recent meeting of "The Athenians" some very interesting papers, prepared by the members were read. Quoting from the paper written by Mrs. George Hunter: "The first societies of women were religious and charitable. These were followed by patriotic societies and organizations of other kinds. At present there exists in the United States a great number of clubs for women which may be considered as falling under the general heads—educational, social and practical. The clubs which may be classified as practical include charitable organizations, societies for civic improvement or for the furthering of schools, libraries, and such organizations as have for their object the securing, by legislation, of improved conditions for working women and children. In 1800 the General Federation of Women's Clubs was formed. There were in the United States at the last enumeration more than 200,000 women belonging to clubs." Get the number? Two hundred thousand! Quite a little army this.

A very interesting paper and one that causes serious thought was that prepared by Mrs. Howe Steele on "The Vocation of Woman." "Woman," says Mrs. Steele, "has found out that, with education and freedom, pursuits of all kinds are open to her and by following these pursuits she can preserve her personal liberty, avoid the grave responsibilities, the almost inevitable sorrows and anxieties which belong to family life. She can choose her friends and change them. She can travel and gratify her tastes and satisfy her personal ambitions. The result is that she frequently is failing to discharge satisfactorily some of the most imperative demands the nation makes upon her. I think it was Longfellow who said: 'Homekeeping hearts are happiest.' Dr. Gilbert said, 'Thru women alone can our faintest dreams become a reality. Woman is the creator of the future souls unborn. Tho she may never be able to speak her ideal, or touch the work she longs to accomplish, yet in the prayer of her soul is the prophecy of her destiny.

Here's to woman the source of all our bliss.
There's foretaste of Heaven in her kiss.
From the Queen upon her throne to the maiden in the
   dairy,
They are all alike in this.'"

LAURA AND THE
YOUNGER GENERATION

Laura Ingalls asked her husband-to-be, Almanzo Wilder, to agree that the word "obey" be deleted from their 1885 wedding service. Almanzo readily agreed, thus setting the tone for the companionable sixty-four years of married life the Wilders shared. They worked as a team throughout the business of farming. If a new horse was needed, Laura and Almanzo discussed the matter. If a venture with sheep raising was considered, they both studied the prospects and planned together. Laura's earnings, together with Almanzo's, helped to buy more land for their Rocky Ridge Farm. Living with such companionable teamwork, Laura found the feminist movement of the early 1900's both radical and sometimes ludicrous.

Laura Wilder's long experience as a farmwife made her an ideal source of wisdom on the subject of women's role in agriculture, a subject on which she had passionately held views. When McCall's Magazine *launched a series of articles exploring the lives of women married to ministers, doctors, artisans, and artists, Laura was asked to write about being a farmer's wife by* McCall's *editor Bessie Beatty, who was a San Francisco friend of Rose's and who knew of the Wilder family and their many years on Rocky Ridge Farm.*

The June 1919 appearance of Laura's article in McCall's *marked her first appearance in a national publication. Her byline was transformed from "Mrs. A. J. Wilder" to "Laura Ingalls*

Wilder" for the first time. "I hope McCall's *comes to Mansfield,"
Rose wrote to Laura of this journalistic triumph. "What a leap of
surprise and awe they will take when they see your name in it!"
Laura's musings on the role of farmwife allowed her to pass along
to a younger generation of women her strong beliefs in farm
women's independence and partnership.*

WHOM WILL YOU MARRY?

Elizabeth came out from town this morning to talk over a
problem with me. I was kneading bread, and because twenty-
five years of it have not taught me to like this part of
the work of a farmer's wife, I had put the bread pan near the
kitchen window where I could look up now and then at
the clean, cool beauty of the budding oak trees. So I saw
Elizabeth as she came up the south slope between the gray
tree trunks, and I thought she looked like a redbird in her
bright sweater and cap.

I felt a twinge of envy. I thought how glad I would be if
I could get out into the spring woods. We always forget our
own compensations in looking at others who have joys that
we have not. But by the time I had opened the door to
Elizabeth and had her in by the stove taking off her muddy
rubbers, the envy was gone. It is a poor life that does not
teach us to shed envy as a duck sheds raindrops, and,
besides, I saw that Elizabeth was troubled.

There was a time when I would have been ashamed to
receive Elizabeth, a banker's granddaughter, in the farm
kitchen. Farm kitchens are not like city kitchenettes, nor

even like the white-painted, muslin-curtained kitchens that some of the town people have. All the work of a farm centers in the farmer's wife's kitchen. I skim milk, make butter, and cook bran mashes for the chickens and potato parings for the hogs in mine. A big iron pot of parings was steaming on the stove when Elizabeth came in.

I may as well admit that Elizabeth, in her dainty, gay clothes, was out of place in my kitchen. Twenty-five years ago, when I was her age, I would have hustled her into the front room and entertained her there, feeling embarrassed because my rag carpet was not Wilton and my furniture was not mahogany. The bread would have waited until she was gone, and if the family ate sourish bread for a week, I would have felt it was not my fault.

But this morning I gave her a kitchen chair and went on kneading, thumping the dough and sprinkling flour over the breadboard while she talked. Good bread is my pride now, rather than Wilton rugs, and I have found that friendliness not genuine in a kitchen is not improved by a parlor.

"Jim's coming home next week," Elizabeth said.

"That's good!" I answered, heartily, for I had watched that romance from the time Elizabeth was in pigtails till the day Jim went away in khaki. But Elizabeth's tone made it clear enough that Jim's coming back brought a little doubt to her mind.

"Would—would you be a farmer's wife if you had the chance to live your life over again?" she asked in that breathless rush in which girls blurt out things they have been thinking about for a long time. "I wanted to talk to you about it. Jim says he wants to buy a farm when he comes back. He says he doesn't want to go into the bank again. I don't know what to do about it. I don't know whether I want to be a farmer's wife or not. Would you, if you were me? I guess I could talk him out of it, but—"

I had no doubt she could talk him out of it. Giving advice to Elizabeth seemed to me a heavy responsibility, though the advice we older women give girls now had not the weight it had when I was a girl. It seems to me that girls nowadays handle their lives and the lives of their husbands with much more assurance than we used to. Elizabeth is really the one who is deciding Jim's future, as well as her own.

In my girlhood we had, one might say, the right of veto in some things in our own lives; we married the man who asked us, or we did not marry him. But now girls make their own laws, and, to an astonishing extent, their own husbands' after they have married them.

While I talked to Elizabeth and kneaded the bread, I thought of many things I did not say. Many persons think that a farmer, and, of course, his wife are isolated from the current of affairs in the nation, but sometimes I think we have a better viewpoint on them because we are farther away. The mail carrier brings out our papers and magazines in the morning, and after the chores are done, I usually have a few minutes to run down to the mailbox and bring them up. During the day, I snatch a glance at them now and then, and after chores are done at night, we sit by the fire and read and talk. We have a great deal of time for thinking at our work and for making our own opinions about the happenings in the world.

So Elizabeth's question seemed to me to mean more than the problem of one girl. I thought of Secretary Lane's plan for placing returning soldiers on farms, and I thought how badly our country needs good farmers and good farm conditions. I thought of the million dollars asked by the Senate Committee on Public Lands for making surveys of farms for soldiers, and I thought of all the girls and women whose opinions mean far more in the matter than any decision of any Senate committee.

There must be a great many of them who, like Elizabeth, are undecided because of their ignorance of the real conditions of life on a farm, and nothing I have ever read seems to tell the truth about these conditions.

There has been a great deal of pity spent on the farmer's wife, and a great deal of condescending effort has been spent to educate her, while, on the other hand, some very pleasant and poetic things have been written about country life. But I have never seen it pointed out that the farm woman's life combines the desires of the "modern woman" with all the advantages and traditions of homekeeping.

On the farm, a woman may have both economic independence and a home life as perfect as she cares to make it. Farm women have always been wage earners and partners in their husband's business. Such a creature as the woman parasite has never been known among us. Perhaps this is one reason why "feminism" has never greatly aroused us.

It has been rather amusing to farm women to read flaring headlines announcing the fact that women are at last coming into their own, that the younger ones at least can now become self-supporting. About the woman past forty there seems to be a little doubt in the papers. But the woman past forty on the farm is still sure of her position, even the woman past fifty or sixty.

There is always plenty of self-supporting, self-respecting work for women on the farm, even though their youth is gone, and the work is within the shelter and quiet security of their own homes. While the discussion for and against women in business has been raging over the country, farm women have always been businesswomen, and no one has protested against it. No one has even noticed it.

Yet I remember well my husband's mother, undisputed head of her household and fully a partner in all the business of the northern Minnesota farm, where I lived for a few months many years ago. She was not a "feminist"; I never heard the words "economic independence" on her lips, and when her daughter, who went to the city and worked in an office, came back to talk of these things, she listened with an indulgent smile. She was too busy to bother her head with such notions, she said. But her husband was never so rash as to sell a herd of hogs or turn meadowland into cornfields without consulting her, and the butter money went into her own purse without a question.

Perhaps the reason this economic value of farm women

has gone unnoticed is because they have taken the advice the small boy gave the hen. When he heard her wildly cackling to announce that she had laid an egg, he exclaimed, "Aw, shut up! What's the use of making such a fuss? You couldn't help it!"

It is true that a farmer's wife can never stop contributing her share to the success of the farm without ruining her husband's business as well. Many times when the churning had to be done and the hens fed, I have felt like running away into the woods, "just to walk and to walk and to stun my soul and amaze it—a day with the stone and the sparrow and every marvelous thing." And I have felt that the life of a parasite woman has its attractions. But it lacks certain sturdy

Laura on Rocky Ridge Farm. Horses were always of great interest to her and to Almanzo; one of her special pleasures was breaking a colt.

virtues that are good for a woman to have.

Women in the cities have tried the parasite life, and it appears that they do not like it. Yet, in the city, conditions inevitably pull married women into economic dependence and partial idleness.

It is not good for any living creature to be idle. A horse that does not work becomes unmanageable and fractious in his stall; he begins eating the wood of the manger, which is not a good thing for a horse to do. Hens, if they are to be kept healthy, must be kept busy, and every good poultry raiser gives them straw to scratch, so that they may earn part of their food by good, honest toil. I think it is not unreasonable to suppose that women, too, must use their energies to some purpose, good or bad, and no woman can make a success of her marriage if she uses her energies in eating the wood of the manger.

Yet, if, in order to avoid the restlessness and uneasiness that go with idleness, the city woman works outside her home, her business interests and occupations pull away from the home life and from marriage.

A species of business rivalry enters into the relations of herself and her husband, and, if she is successful, she has a pride in her pay envelope which is only equaled by her husband's jealousy of it. A man is perhaps slower to adapt himself to new things than a woman, or it may be that there is some deep, possessive instinct in him that resents any rival in the attention of the woman he loves. Combating this feeling in her husband gives a woman a sense of power, and nothing tears the delicate fabric of intimacy between two persons so surely as this sense of power in one and of futile protest in the other.

With separated interests, differing ambitions, a different set of business friends, and a jealous rivalry between them, it is no wonder that so many fine men and women in the cities are finding marriage impossible. The divorce court makes legal a separation which already exists, and their marriage is a failure, whatever their business successes may be.

It is in the cities that the divorce statistics pile higher with every year. Divorce is rare in the country.

The farm woman's economic independence pulls in the direction of making her marriage a success. Her interests and those of her husband are the same; their success is a mutual success of which each may be equally proud. In the event of a threatened failure, their interests still hold them together, instead of pulling them apart, and failure may often be averted because of the simple fact that two heads are better than one.

A farmer's wife may and should be—I may almost say must be—her husband's partner in the business, and she may be this without detracting from the home life.

Meals on time; the surplus of garden and orchard preserved; meats properly cured at butchering time; the young creatures on the farm cared for as only a woman has the patience to care for them; work in the dairy and with the poultry contribute very largely to the success of the average farmer.

The farm woman does such work as this at home, without bringing any alien influence to bear upon the home life. A farmer never becomes jealous of his wife's success with the poultry, however large a check it brings in, nor does she feel that it makes her independent of him.

I cannot say there is no rivalry between them, remembering that only last year our farm was the scene of a long and serious contest. Over the supper table one night my husband and I found ourselves suddenly disputing vigorously over the relative value of hens and cows as money-makers.

I suppose I was bitter about the hens. For a week I had been coaxing them to lay, by every means in my power, and they had responded with beautifully bright combs and shining feathers, but not with eggs. Night after night, I came in past the barnyard with the egg basket rattling lightly on my arm, to find brimming milk pails standing by the separator. I contended that cows paid far better than hens.

My husband takes care of the cows, and during the war, it seemed that the stock might as well be living on minted gold as on mill feed. The summer had been dry, and we faced a winter in which we might have to buy hay. He was strongly prejudiced in favor of hens.

The argument finally became a contest. Each of us was to keep exact accounts, and at the end of six months we were to compare figures. We played fair, each working to prove the other right by taking the best care of our charges; and when, at last, we held an executive session to determine the results, we found that we were both right. The same time was required to care for three cows as for one hundred hens, and the same profit was made.

That is the kind of business rivalry which lends zest to a year's work on a farm. It also gives point to a bit of conversation between our hired man and a neighbor, which my husband overheard and repeated to me with a twinkle in his eye. The hired man was to be married. Our neighbor, stopping beside the fence to talk, was told the news.

"Married!" he exclaimed. "Why, you can't make a living for yourself!"

"Well," the hired man said cheerfully, "I figure she'll help a little."

I am not saying that the life of a farmer's wife is an easy one. We never get anything for nothing, though we may have almost anything in the world if we are willing to pay the price.

Economic independence is not an easy thing for a woman to earn, even on a farm, and part of the price that must be paid for it is responsibility. A farm woman cannot expect to be full partner in pleasures and profits and not share troubles and labor.

I know one farmer's wife who insists in having a voice in all the farm affairs and then, when things go wrong, blames her husband. She fails in her own part of the work. Her hens never lay; she will not help out in harvesting time, when help is scarce, by feeding the horses or turning the cream separator; she cannot raise a calf nor have the meals ready on time.

Yet she complains because her husband does not make a better living for her.

This woman does not belong on a farm. There are times when a farmer's wife must neglect her own special part of the work and help her husband, in order that the crop may be saved or the livestock cared for. If the farmer is injured or ill, there may be no one but his wife to take over the entire farm management and a large part of the physical labor besides.

Sometimes a woman must work in this way to pay off the mortgage or meet some unexpected loss caused by bad weather, and in that case, she must help or see the business fail utterly. Every farmer's wife who begins her married life with little money must be prepared to meet such emergencies, but the words of Lord Halifax are as true of women as of men. He said: "A difficulty raiseth the spirit of a great man. He hath a mind to wrestle with it and give it a fall. A man's mind must be very low if the difficulty doth not make part of his pleasure."

There is a joy of spirit and a pride of power that come to a farm woman who is fully alive to her opportunities, meeting and solving problems, confronting and overcoming difficulties, refusing to become petty though attending to numberless details, or to be discouraged before threatened disaster. She wins to a valiant courage of the soul, which holds itself above all harassments, serene and unconquered.

Just as the physical labor of a farm exercises and makes strong every part of a woman's body, so the many interests of the farm life, in threads which reach to it from all parts of the world, exercise her mind.

When the price of eggs goes down, with a corresponding cut in the amount of her weekly check, she will want to know the reason why. When there is an increase in the price of cut bone and meat scraps, which she must feed the hens to produce those eggs, she will ask the reason for that.

Why, she will wonder, does the farmer need helpful laws for his business, more than the grocer, or the banker, or the doctor?

Why is it necessary, in spite of all the natural advantages offered by country life, in spite of the real need of our country for more and better farmers, for our government to use all its efforts of persuasion and inducement in order to turn back that tide of movement from the farms to the cities?

These are problems that can be solved, conditions that can be altered only by the wisdom and efforts of the farmers themselves. There is scope here for all that a woman has of intelligence and fine spirit. There is an opportunity here for the woman who will do her part in remaking a world that has been shaken to its foundations by discoveries the war has forced upon us.

Altogether aside from the feeling of independence and security that comes to a woman through her position as a farmer's wife, she has a deep satisfaction in knowing she is not struggling against someone else for advancement; that her success will not be built upon the downfall of others. Her rise to prosperity is not over the broken fortunes or through the suffering or oppression of those weaker than herself.

Instead, by the labor of her hands, she is producing food for humanity and is, in the old and delightful sense, a lady, a "bread-giver."

Farm life has its ample compensations for all its hardships, and the greatest of these is a sense and enjoyment of the real values of life.

These are not the modern improvements of which we hear so much, the telephone, the rural free delivery, the automobile, and the labor-saving machinery, which are bringing many of the city's advantages to the country. They are not even the beauties of nature, which give so much daily joy and always help over the hard places.

The real values of farm life are simplicity, money honestly earned, difficulties overcome, service lovingly given, respect deserved; in short, the exercise of physical, mental, and spiritual muscles until a rounded, complete, individual character is built.

These are the things I have learned in twenty-five years as a farmer's wife, and so, turning to Elizabeth this morning, I tried to say to her something like this:

"Whether or not you are fitted for the life of a farmer's wife depends on what you want to get from your marriage.

"If you want ease, unearned luxuries, selfish indulgence, a silken-cushioned, strawberries-and-cream life, do not marry a man who will be a farmer.

"If you want to give, as well as to take; if you want to be your husband's full partner in business and in homemaking;

if you can stand on your own feet and face life as a whole, the troubles and difficulties and the real joys and growth that come from them; if you want an opportunity to be a fine, strong, free woman, then you are fitted for the life of a farmer's wife, to be his partner, the providence of your own little world of the farm and bread-giver to humanity, the true lady of the world."

While Laura would not have called herself a feminist, she was clearly a strong advocate of equal partnership between wives and husbands. She was also sympathetic to the turn-of-the-century phenomenon of the "bachelor girl." In their shortened skirts and shirtwaist blouses, this army of young women filled dozens of positions in the workforces of cities and small towns across America, and Laura wholeheartedly supported their right to earn their living. In fact, her own daughter, Rose Wilder, was a bachelor girl. In 1904, Rose was supporting herself as a Kansas City telegraph operator, and Laura was proud of her.

In her conventional role as a farmwife living near a small town, Laura passionately and humorously examined the changes in the life of women and the status of single women in this essay, written around the time of World War I.

OUR DARING DAUGHTERS

The ladies of the Methodist Episcopal Aid Society were serving dinner, at the noon hour, in the room over Reynolds' general store where they were holding their annual bazaar.

I had been late in getting there and was examining the

articles that had been donated for the sale and were pinned to the sheets tacked along the walls. There were aprons, many and varied, sunbonnets, boudoir caps, dust caps, dresser scarfs, pincushions, and towels of every description from plain hem stitched ones to those elaborately hand embroidered or trimmed with hand made, knit lace.

Handkerchiefs were pinned in all the odd corners and small framed pictures were hung here and there. Each of these articles had its price tag attached and it had been a busy morning for those in charge of the sale.

Just now attention was centered on the long tables covered with white cloths which were set down the middle of the room. On the tables were plates of white bread and of brown bread, dishes of butter and of pickles and salads of different kinds. People were coming and going at these tables while the cashier of the Aid Society hovered near, collecting the price of the dinner.

In an improvised kitchen, at the back of the room, the older women were dishing up the food on plates which white-aproned girls carried to the diners at the tables. Portions of baked beans, fried or roast or boiled chicken, with gravy, mashed potatoes, candied sweet potatoes and boiled ham were put on each plate. A cup of coffee and a piece of pie were also served to each guest.

"What kind of pie have you, Ada?" asked Mr. G., a large blond man who was very fond of good things to eat.

"Apple, peach, blackberry, cherry, gooseberry, chocolate, cream and pumpkin," answered Ada.

"Any lemon?" inquired Mr. G. in a lowered voice and with a knowing look. And with a nod and a smile Ada went back to the kitchen.

"Where'd you hide that lemon pie, Sarah?" she said quietly to the gray haired president of the Aid Society who was at the pie table.

"Who'd you want it for?" asked Sarah in the same low tone. "Oh, for Mr. G.! It's under that pan. Cut a small piece for I want some of it left for myself."

As I watched this little by-play, a shrill voice came unexpectedly from beside me.

"Well how are you?" it said. "Why don't you ever come over? And how is Rose? I heard she had got a divorce. Is that true?"

I was fairly caught and knew that I was in for an unpleasant few minutes. I murmured an affirmative answer and the unpleasantly loud voice caught me up quickly.

"You say she has a divorce! Well! There it is again! What for? And now she will have to earn her own living!"

It was a shock to hear voiced again the old idea that only women who were without husbands earned their own livings and as I caught the once familiar thought I realized with surprise that I was of the same age as the woman talking.

Unconsciously I had always treated her with the respect one shows one's elders—or did—Why! that very attitude placed me a generation back from the present.

What was it I heard a young woman say only the other

day? "There is nothing about gray hairs as gray hairs to command respect."

When I was a girl no young person would have said such a thing even had they dared think it, but I fully agreed with her, having, I think, grown more honest and less sentimental. If one has lived long enough to acquire gray hair and has done nothing more to command respect than to let the years pass by why should youth be expected to feel reverence?

But having grown tired of my hesitation, the woman at my elbow asked again sharply, "What did she get a divorce for?"

Her tone was one of reproof as though I were in some way guilty and I felt very helpless for I saw how far I had strayed with the younger people from the standards of her and my youth.

How could I explain to any one who asked with that tone of voice, that the persons of whom we were speaking had obtained a divorce because they were absolutely uncongenial, because they "got on each other's nerves" to such an extent that their companionship was ruining the character of both. I was saved from the annoying situation by a whirlwind of children that came dancing across the room.

"Oh, Mama says will you come cut bread? They need more help," cried the little girl in the lead and so I made my escape.

"And now she will have to make her own living," I muttered as I fled.

That was the way people used to think about it, I

Rose at nineteen, while working as a telegrapher in Kansas City.

remembered and could feel myself flush. It was humiliating to think that a woman had once been expected to give herself body and soul in exchange for her living; that her patient, hard work as housekeeper, cook, washerwoman, nursemaid and general maid of all work had not been considered of any money value.

I glanced back at the woman I was leaving and noticed the signs of old age and housekeeping cares.

"What have you done with your youth and health and strength, if you have not earned your living," I thought?

"Why is it that you women always want your daughters to marry?" a girl once asked me. The reason is very simple. When we older women were girls almost any kind of a marriage was a happier lot than that of an unmarried woman, for opportunities for an independent, single life were few.

The choice of careers for women then lay between being a hired girl, a dressmaker, or a school teacher. The girl who stayed at home and failed to marry usually became a hired girl without pay in the home of some married sister or brother. That was not a pleasant life and naturally girls preferred to marry and have homes of their own; to care for their own, instead of other peoples' children, and to work in their own kitchens.

Besides all this, "Old Maid" was a term of reproach for the implication was always there that if a girl remained unmarried she had not been found desirable.

Jennie Chase was perilously near the line between a young lady and an old maid. She was small and nervous. We called her cross. She worked hard, for living with her married brother she had plenty to do though she drew no salary.

She had outgrown the younger girls, who did not care

Laura in October 1906; this photograph was taken while she was on a visit to Rose in Kansas City.

for her company and used to laugh at her efforts to "catch a beau" and she did not belong with the married crowd, because she had no husband.

Finally she married a very unattractive man and one of the younger girls remarked, "Jennie will die happy now, for she can have 'Mrs' written on her tombstone and maybe she can have a new hat."

The same reasons that made marriage so desirable were a great influence in keeping a woman married. Divorce was almost unknown. The position of a divorced woman was even more unpleasant than that of an old maid. Besides the difficulties of earning her living, she was classed with the women who wore false hair and powdered. She was just as bad.

A family moved into our town, a man, a woman and two little boys. Soon a rumor followed them that Mrs. Hays had been divorced, that Mr. Hays was not the father of the boys. It was talked about quietly in lowered voices. One woman said in my hearing, "Well, they may be married, but the father of those boys is alive and I will never treat her as though she were a respectable woman so long as he is."

And so carefully hidden by we girls, under sentiment, romance and coquetishness, was the fear that we might not be chosen, that we might be left to become old maids.

It was a matter of pride in my family that in all the range of connections no girl had failed to be married at eighteen years; an old maid in the family was unknown.

I was married in time to keep up the family reputation but I did not follow precedent in the manner of it. My hero of the fast team and the sleigh rides did not "endow" me with his "worldly goods" with the string of the word "obey" attached to them, nor did I promise him my soul, with mental reservations, by the use of that word.

This was a daring innovation, but thanks to the old minister who performed the ceremony, we started even each alike promising to love, honor and respect the other, which is a large enough promise in all conscience when made at eighteen.

Like all girls of all times, I had dreamed of the prince who would one day come and claim me, but my dreams all ended there. All the romances we ever read ended with marriage. The only thing left to do was to live happily ever after. It seemed to be the general opinion that when a girl was successfully married there would be nothing in her life afterward worth making a story about.

Greatly to my surprise, I found that with my marriage the story had hardly begun and since then I have found life daily more engrossing and worth while as I have watched and experienced the changes in the life and ideas of women.

Now that my own girl is grown up, I can sympathize with my Mother and I realize that whatever our mistakes have been the younger generation is certain to discover them and we may safely leave our revenge in the hands of the generation following them, for just as Fairyland is the native country of Childhood, so Youth lives in the state of Rebellion and under the assumption that whatever is, is wrong proceeds at once to make it right.

It is a joy to behold how blithely young folks go at this task and surprising what they accomplish.

The little town near which I live today is proud of its modern improvements, its graded school and churches; its electric lights, ice plant, telephones, automobiles and young woman city treasurer.

I go to the bank to transact business and am waited on by a charming and businesslike young woman. At the post-office I receive courteous attention from the chief clerk, again a young woman. At the newspaper office I find the busy editor and his business partner equally busy, smiling and efficient, who is also the partner of his joys and sorrows, his wife. While in town I pay my telephone bill to the woman owner and manager of the telephone system, unless she has driven her car out to inspect the line. The girls who wish to work out doors put on overalls and go out into the fields when they are needed and no tight laced corset hinders the freedom of their movements.

But still our girls think the opportunities are not good enough in the home town and many go to the cities to find better as a matter of course.

My daughter Rose made her start in the city as a telegrapher, but soon left that for the more congenial work of reporter for a daily paper and now, after only a few years is making a national reputation as a writer of books and for the leading magazines.

Sadie started in at home as a clerk in the drug store and now she is manager of a city drug store on a large salary.

Vivian began as a stenographer and is now the confidential secretary of a man of wealth and position.

When Mable married Dick it was not because he would rescue her from an unpleasant life of dependence for she was already independent and could marry or remain single without in any way affecting her position and when Hattie left her husband and came home, if there was any difference, she was treated with just a little more consideration and kindness than usual.

They all powder their noses shamelessly in public when they become shiny or wear extra hair when they wish with an assurance which says the queen can do no wrong. And it does my heart good to see it too for it is to me a sign of openness and candor, of an independence of thought and action, of the lessening of that cringing fear of what people will say and I hope a growth of the principle of holding one's self strictly accountable for what one does, letting none of the responsibility rest on others. Such girls no longer excite criticism.

I was once bluntly asked by the mother of Stella, whose daughter was a girlhood chum of my own girl, "Is it true what I heard about Rose, that she is now smoking cigarettes? Isn't it a shame!" exclaimed Stella's mother. "It will set the fashion of course and with the girls all taking to smoking, I don't know what will become of the human race."

Stella blew an imaginary wreath of smoke from her lips and deliberately winked at me over her mother's head.

"I don't think it will do any harm," I said. "My grandmother smoked a pipe in a very dainty, ladylike way, if yours didn't, without a doubt she dipped snuff and we're here so why worry. Young women who smoke today are only doing as their great grandmothers did fifty or a hundred years ago." But don't imagine I mean to say that the human race is going backward. Some follies come back now and then, such as the smoking of cigarettes and the little sister of the tie-back skirt, but these are only superficial.

Somewhere I have read that humanity is ascending in the scale of life in a spiral form, traveling around in circles but with each circle a little higher than the one preceding.

I love to think of this circular ascension as being like the process of skimming milk with my cream separator which skims by centrifugal force, the milk spinning around and around flinging the waste products off as the cream rises higher and higher until it is saved.

Thus while the human race may be traveling more or less in a circle some mighty centrifugal force is separating all that is of value from the waste and it is rising higher and higher in each generation.

When the older generation comes to believe that nothing of theirs which is worth saving will be lost and when the younger generation learns that while new friends, new ways and new ideas may be worth trying out, those that have stood the test of use are not to be lightly cast aside, then great things will happen in the world, for almost nothing would be impossible to the wisdom and patience gained by experience joined with the daring and courage of youth.

"I never graduated from anything and only attended high school two terms," said Laura Ingalls Wilder regretfully when asked about her education. Prepared with that limited education and her own natural abilities, however, Laura taught school, became a writer, and was known as one of Mansfield's resident intellectuals. She was always strongly pro-education and deplored instances of farm children's missing school because their labor was needed at home. She believed that a generation of ill-educated children would become a generation of adults who would not be useful or effective "citizens of the nation."

In 1923, Laura was asked to attend the Wright County School Fair at Hartville. She recorded her impressions for the Missouri Ruralist, *proudly noting that farm children and town children had worked together to produce impressive results in their learning achievements.*

THE FAIRS THAT BUILD MEN

We accept, without thinking about it, the fact that happy nations do not appear in history. But only lately I have realized that events of greatest importance are least noticed, even while they are occurring under our very eyes.

I realized this when I walked down the steps of the Hartville high school building, thinking of the fair I had just seen and comparing it with others I remembered. There was the unforgettable World's Fair in San Francisco, the several great state fairs at Sedalia, the land congress fairs, county fairs, stock fairs, poultry fairs—all of them interesting and admirable. But this fair I had just seen, this small fair unknown outside Wright county, mentioned only in the Hartville papers, seemed to me more important than any of them.

The great World's Fairs show what has been builded by nations: the small rural school fairs are building the nation itself, for the training which these children are getting in cooperation and honorable competition will make of them useful and possibly great citizens of the nation and the world. It means much to a child, in character building, to learn to be an honest winner or a good loser in whatever contest he takes part, whether it be a World War or a poultry show.

This fair was a fair of children, and—under guidance—by and for children. School children made nearly half of the record-breaking attendance of 2,500 who crowded the school building and grounds.

The children of the Hartville School cooking class served luncheon to them all, and were kept rather more than comfortably busy preparing the quantities of toothsome dishes. If it had been possible to use the food exhibited there would easily have been an abundant supply of the best quality. It made one's mouth water to gaze on the quantities of beautiful canned fruit and rosy-cheeked apples, the nuts and grains and vegetables.

The growth, care and selection of all these exhibits must have made farm work, thru the year, intensely interesting to the pupils of the 24 schools represented.

There were 44 varieties of canned fruit exhibited by New Mountain Dale School. There were 15 varieties of grasses and 78 kinds of native woods shown by Rodgers School. There were 18 varieties of forest leaves collected by the Hall School. These exhibits were in addition to those of the regular school work, agricultural and manual training displays, among which was a special model of a milking stool designed by one of the Rodgers School class.

Little Creek School brought 27 varieties of forest leaves, 21 varied grains, 22 kinds of seeds, 14 species of insects, 10 noxious weeds, 70 kinds of native woods. Little Creek School by this astounding total won second prize for exhibits.

Pleasant Hill School carried off first prize with a large display of turnips, pumpkins, potatoes, melons, grains, grasses, weeds, knots, agricultural maps, general school work, fancy work, patchwork, potted flowers, 37 varieties of canned fruit, 11 varieties of apples, a roomful of chickens, and a calf, with an overflow into the school yard of two pens of hogs.

Blanchard School won third prize for exhibits.

Lone Star School, with 100 per cent attendance, accompanied by their entire school board, for the second time won the attendance prize.

The teachers of these schools, Emmett Jones, Pleasant Hill; J. M. Vestal, Little Creek; Homer Smith, Blanchard; and Mrs. James Shelby, Lone Star, certainly deserve honorable mention. And what a training all these rural teachers have been giving their pupils in observance of the world around them, in seeing and knowing leaf and weed and insect and all the varied, interesting things on the farm.

Reading contests and singing contests were features of

the last day of the fair. The song contest was won by Pleasant Hill School. Glenette McGowan, of Blanchard School carried off the prize in the reading contest.

Basket ball and other athletic games, played on the campus in a spirit of friendly rivalry and good temper, were a pleasure to witness.

Good speaking during the fair added much to the interest of the occasion.

In the exhibits and school work, health, agriculture, poultry and dairy farming were emphasized and much interest was shown by farm folks attending, in the definite lessons presented on feeding dairy cows, poultry and hogs by Professor Hess's vocational class and also in the soil exhibit showing methods of fertilization and testing for the need of lime, while the model poultry house and the model farm with its impressive lesson in the necessity of crop rotation to maintain soil fertility were much talked about.

All this can not fail in affecting for the better the farming methods of the county and being an education for parents as well as children.

The Wright County School Fair for 1923 was a remarkable success and much of the credit for this is due Professor Hess of the Hartville Schools, University Extension workers and County Superintendent Ray Wood, who with his hard working rural teachers, backed by the business and professional men of Hartville, worked together for that object.

EARLY MEMORIES

*"I have always lived a very busy life," said Laura Ingalls Wilder
as she looked back on the pioneering days with her parents, Charles
and Caroline Ingalls, and the homesteading and farming years
with her husband, Almanzo. She was not afraid of physical labor;
when it was needed, she drove farm machinery in the wheat fields
of Dakota Territory, helped to fell timber in the Ozark hills, and
overcame privations and primitive conditions to be a model homemaker wherever she was. Although she was often busy from dawn
to sunset, her thoughts on life, her memories of frontier life, and her
always-expanding personal philosophies were constantly with her.
Often, in the evening lamplight, or by the crackling fireplace of
her Rocky Ridge farmhouse, she wrote down her memories, which
convey her deep and abiding love for her early days, and her sad-
ness at their passing. To anyone who reads these quick yet heartfelt
sketches, it is not surprising that Laura eventually turned her
hand at writing the unforgettable story of her childhood in the
Little House books. One of her earliest autobiographical sketches is
this one about her father.*

FIRST MEMORIES OF FATHER

Oh yes, the pictures that hang in my memory. . . . The first
sign of approaching old age has come to me for I love to
look back upon them. I am without wrinkles and with but
three gray hairs (I counted them this morning) and still the
times and places have so changed that you wish to look

upon my memory pictures. The first is of my Father always. My first memory is of his eyes, so clear and sharp and blue. Those eyes that could look unerringly along a rifle barrel in the face of a bear or a pack of wolves and yet were so tender as they rested on his Caroline (my mother) or me when I was sick as I frequently was. His hair was thick and fine and he wore a tawny beard. He was the swiftest skater in the neighborhood, a strong swimmer and could travel miles on his snow shoes or tramp all day through the woods without fatigue. His arms were so strong he could break down a door with one blow of his naked fist and his strong arms carried me many a night when I was sick and restless. I can hear his measured steps yet, back and forth across the floor, feel the comfort of those strong arms and hear his soothing, "there, there", and also his kind voice saying "No Caroline, you lie down and sleep." The feeling, the voice and the dim light over the log wall make a picture that will never fade.

All Father needed to make him happy was his family, a new, wild country to live in or travel over, good hunting and fishing, some traps, his gun, two good horses hitched to a rain-proof covered wagon and his violin.

I am not sure but I should have put the violin first and the family second and I know that its place was second only to the family with us all.

It made merry with us when we were glad, it sympathized with us when we were sad, it gave us paeans of praise when we had been good or successful and acted as a father confessor when we had been bad.

When Father played on his violin in the twilight, I could no more help confessing, if I had been naughty during the day than I could keep from giving my Father and Mother the love that welled up in my heart, at times, until it was a positive pain.

Many a time I have gone to sleep at night, after being forgiven for some childish sin, with the kiss of my Mother warm on my lips and the music of Father's violin lulling me to dreams.

At times I hear it yet, in that land between waking and sleeping just before I fall asleep. Dear old love songs, "The Blue Juniata," "Kitty Wells," "Annie Laurie" and "Highland Mary." The songs of home and country—"Home Sweet Home," "Bonnie Doon," "Columbia The Gem Of the Ocean," as well as those of lighter vein, "Yankee Doodle," "Pop! Goes The Weasel," "Old Zip Coon," "The Irish Washerwoman," "The Devil's Dream"—dance music to make the toes tingle.

Then as twilight deepened into night, for a good night blessing, came the quaint old hymn tunes, "Come Ye Soldiers Of The Cross," "Shall I be carried to the skies on flowery beds of ease while others fought to win the prize or sailed through bloody seas?" "Rock Of Ages" and "There Is A Land Of Pure Delight."

Whatever religion, romance and patriotism I have I owe largely to the violin and my Father playing in the twilight. I am sure that when I come to die, if Father might only be playing for me I should be wafted straight to heaven on the

Laura had Pa's fiddle photographed in 1943 for an article written about her in The Horn Book *magazine.*

strains of "The Sweet By And By," for the pearly gates would surely open.

Christmas during Laura's childhood, though generally spare by necessity and also by the custom of the times, was nevertheless the stuff of fond memory. Indeed, some of the most memorable chapters in the Little House books are of Christmas celebrations. Simple though these joyous occasions were, they left a lasting impression. While she was writing for the Missouri Ruralist, *Laura submitted "Christmas Bells of Long Ago," which communicated her nostalgic warm feelings for the holidays of her girlhood.*

Christmas Bells of Long Ago

I sit at eve' in the fire-light,
Once more 'tis Christmas time:
And there falls on the ear of my fancy,
A far off silvery chime.
Listen! Do you hear them ringing
Faint and far, so sweet and low,
Like elfin chimes of fairyland,
Christmas bells of long ago?

I long for the friends of childhood,
Goblin and elf and sprite!
I want Santa to come to me
As he used, on a Christmas night!
Searching my soul for the reason,

Laura, Almanzo, and Nero, their dog, circa 1930, in their new rock house. It was around this time that Laura first began jotting down memories of her childhood.

I sit in the firelight's glow.
Why will not Santa come to me,
Over the fields of snow?

The rush and the roar of living
Dulls childhood's listening ears:
And the simple faith of childhood
Is lost through all the years.
Reason has banished mystery,
For hard hearts will not believe,
So that even Santa leaves us
To be lonely Christmas Eve'.

But if we listen, we will hear
Soft whispers, among the trees,
And fairy folk, of field and dell,
Still dance adown the breeze—
Once, I heard the bells of Santa
Driving reindeer through the snow
And to night I hear them ringing,
Christmas bells of long ago.

The people who filled Laura's life during her years in De Smet were largely lost to her after she moved to Missouri. These friends from the 1880's generally moved away, as the Wilders did, or were engaged, as the Wilders were, in the struggle to raise families and create homes. But Laura would bring them all back to life in the pages of her books Little Town on the Prairie *and*

These Happy Golden Years. *Long before she wrote those stories, however, she wrote the following poem.*

Little Town of Memory

Oh little town! In memory
How sweet your voices singing:
I see your faces bright and gay:
I hear your sleigh bells ringing.

This little town has disappeared
It vanished with the years
A different town with the same name
In the same place appears—
A large town a modern town—
And my memory of this little town
I lay away with tears.

Oh little town of memory
I hear your voices singing
I see your faces bright and gay
I hear your sleighbells ringing—
It all has gone beyond recall
Its music fades away.

THE LITTLE HOUSE AUTHOR

After many years as an essay writer and columnist, in her sixties Laura finally turned to writing down her vivid memories of her pioneer childhood. What began as a single book grew, with Rose's encouragement and editorial advice, to a series of eight books published in Laura's lifetime. She wrote these books to record and preserve a way of life that was ending, and to let the younger generation know what life had been like for those intrepid settlers. Little did Laura know that her books would make her name a household word.

Though she was known in local circles as a fine journalist, Laura was completely unknown to the book world. In fact, it was Rose whose work was well known. Rose had published three books with Harper & Brothers and was widely considered to be a fine writer. To help launch her mother's career and introduce her to the national public, Harper asked Rose to profile Laura. She did so, writing the following biography for promotional purposes. Rose's profile became Laura's first introduction to book reviewers, booksellers, and readers.

MY MOTHER, LAURA INGALLS WILDER

My mother was born in the little log house described in *Little House in the Big Woods.* That is to say, the Big Woods of Wisconsin near Lake Pepin in the Mississippi. But she says she doesn't remember that. Her first memories are of a venture into Indian Territory, some fifty miles south of what is

Rose Wilder Lane in a New York publishing office around 1938.

now Independence, Kansas; she was then about three. Her father was a pioneer hunter, trapper, and Indian fighter. He was one of the founders of the town that is now De Smet, South Dakota; put up the first building on the town-site, founded the Congregational church there, was Justice of the Peace and acted as such before the country was organized.

The family lived there through the remembered Hard Winter, 1880–1881, when there were no trains from October to May and the town of about 100 people was snowed in, cut off from help, used up all supplies and was without light, food and fuel. My father, with another boy, risked his life driving forty miles to get a little seed-wheat from a farmer known to have some; women ground it in coffee-mills and the people lived on small rations of it made into mush. Later, illegally because she was not yet sixteen, my mother taught school; she passed the examinations triumphantly and by connivance with the school directors the examiners omitted to ask her age. She married my father when she was eighteen. My father took up homestead and tree-claim. He raised wheat. There were seven successive years of crop failures, ending when I was three; the land produced a bumper crop that year, which was to pay all the debts and begin prosperity for the family. But in July, the day before the threshers were coming, a hail-storm pounded the whole crop into the ground. I remember standing with my mother at the kitchen window and watching it. Later they bought forty acres of uncleared hill land in Missouri, mortgaged for $200 and paid $100 for it, this being literally every dollar my parents had.

Since then they have lived on this farm. It is now 200 acres of pasture, meadow-land and woodlots, an equipped dairy farm, with three houses on it, completely modern even to electric ranges and oil-burning steam heat.

My mother has done all the work a farmer's wife usually does; she's an expert cook, dairy-maid and poultry raiser. She also organized women's clubs, farm-clubs and farm-women's clubs, all around through southwestern Missouri, and organized and was for twelve years secretary-treasurer of the Mansfield Farm Loan Association, a branch of the Federal Farm Loan Bank. She handled all the detail of lending to farmers in this country, in small amounts, nearly a million dollars of government money, and the association was the banner one in its territory. As long as she was handling it, it had a record of not one bad loan and not one delay in payments.

She is now about sixty-five, small, very pretty, dresses more in the mode than I do; she has very blue eyes and white hair cut short. She has an intense interest in politics; reads all current articles on politics and economics and still from old habit follows with interest stock-yard reports and grain-market quotations. Her favorite fiction writer is John Buchan.*

Little House in the Big Woods is her first book and she is tremendously excited about the publication. Incidentally, she

* Buchan (Baron Tweedsmuir) was a Scottish-born author of over sixty books. Laura especially liked his adventure tales, which included *Greenmantle, The Thirty-Nine Steps,* and *Prester John.*

and my father are still perfectly crazy about each other. And her gingerbread is famous throughout the country. She will not have a servant and does all her own housework.

A dozen years after Rose Wilder Lane penned Laura Ingalls Wilder's first publicity sketch, she was again asked for impressions of her mother for an article in The Horn Book *magazine. During those intervening years, from 1931 to 1943, "Mrs. A. J. Wilder" had rapidly been transformed into the celebrated author Laura Ingalls Wilder. The modest beginnings of* Little House in the Big Woods, *published in the depths of the Depression, developed into the eight-volume* Little House *series. By the time* These Happy Golden Years *appeared in 1943, the books were already considered classics. (A ninth book,* The First Four Years, *had been written, but it was not published until 1971.)*

Readers were always eager to know "what happened next" to Laura, Almanzo, and their families. Writing from her home in Danbury, Connecticut, during the 1950's, Rose wrote this word portrait of her mother, which sheds some light on Laura's writing habits. In a postscript, Rose cautioned that she herself must not be mentioned. "It must be exasperating," Rose noted, "to be so frequently tagged, 'Rose Wilder Lane's mother.' After a life like hers, during a life like hers, she can stand on her own feet."

SHE CAN STAND ON HER OWN FEET

She's the serious, wide-eyed girl now almost shyly hidden under a surface quickness and sparkle. She's little, about five feet tall, has very small hands and feet, and large, violet-blue

About the Books Themselves

 ☐ **LITTLE HOUSE IN THE BIG WOODS**

Over sixty-five years ago, in a log cabin on the edge of the Big Woods of Wisconsin, Mrs. Wilder spent part of her childhood. "This has a refreshingly genuine and life-like quality . . . Christmas, churning and butter-making, hog-killing, and 'sugaring off' are described with zest and humor. The characters are very much alive and the portrait of Laura's father is drawn with loving care and reality." — *N. Y. Times.* Pictures by Helen Sewell. Ages 8 to 12. Cloth (6¾ x 8½). $2.00.

 ☐ **LITTLE HOUSE ON THE PRAIRIE**

The Ingalls family moved from the Big Woods to Kansas, Indian Territory in those days. Some nights there were wolves, often they saw Indians. As always the family made the best of what they had. They planted, plowed, hunted ducks and turkeys, chopped logs. And at the end of a year they were sorry to leave the cabin on the plains for a new land farther west. Pictures by Helen Sewell. Ages 8 to 12. Cloth (6¾ x 8½). $2.00.

☐ **FARMER BOY**

A year in Almanzo Wilder's boyhood on a big New York state farm over seventy years ago. Almanzo helped with spring planting, with fall threshing, with cutting huge ice blocks and log-hauling in winter. He trained his own team of young twin oxen and won a blue ribbon at the county fair with a giant pumpkin. When spring came again his father gave him Starlight, a beautiful colt, to break in and keep as his own. Pictures by Helen Sewell. Ages 8 to 12. Cloth (6¾ x 8½). $2.00.

☐ **ON THE BANKS OF PLUM CREEK**

When the Ingalls moved to Minnesota they lived in a sod house and Pa built them a beautiful new one of sweet-smelling wood and real laughter window panes. Laura and Mary loved their new life. Of course there were tragedies — the plague of grasshoppers and the blizzard. But there were good things too, the creek to play in, and in the evenings the sweet music of Pa's fiddle. Pictures by Helen Sewell and Mildred Boyle. Ages 8 to 12. Cloth (6¾ x 8½). $2.00.

 ☐ **BY THE SHORES OF SILVER LAKE**

The Ingalls moved next to Dakota Territory in the days of the building of the railroads. Pa was a railroad man until he found a homestead and filed claim. The Ingalls spent the winter in a surveyor's house sixty miles from the nearest neighbor. There was Laura and Mary's thrilling train ride, the attempted payroll robbery, and the Ingalls' happiest Christmas. When spring came Pa put up the first building on the town-site near his claim. And two weeks later there was a brand-new town. Pictures by Helen Sewell and Mildred Boyle. Ages 9 to 13. Cloth (6¾ x 9¾). $2.00.

 ☐ **THE LONG WINTER**

Indian warning said the winter of 1880-81 would be a hard one, so Pa moved his family into town. Blizzards snowed the little town under, cutting off all supplies from the outside. When Christmas had passed and there was a desperate need for food, Almanzo Wilder and another boy made a dangerous trip across the prairie to secure wheat. It was May before the snows melted and the first train got through, bringing the Ingalls' Christmas barrel. Then they had the best and gayest celebration they ever had. Pictures by Helen Sewell and Mildred Boyle. Ages 9 to 13. Cloth (6¾ x 9¾). $2.00.

 ☐ **LITTLE TOWN ON THE PRAIRIE**

Social life soon flourished in the little town — there was a school and a church. Laura went to a wonderful 4th of July celebration, attended her first evening "social"; Almanzo Wilder took her riding behind his dashing team and exchanged the fashionable new "name cards" with her. Things went well with the Ingalls and Mina! Mary was at last able to go to college. At the very end, when Laura was fifteen, she received her teacher's certificate. Pictures by Helen Sewell and Mildred Boyle. Ages 9 to 13. Cloth (6¾ x 9¾). $2.00.

 ☐ **THESE HAPPY GOLDEN YEARS**

In it Laura teaches her first school, before she is sixteen, in an abandoned claim shanty twelve miles from home. In the summer Mary is home from college. Laura helps the dressmaker in town, and Almanzo breaks colts to drive. There are sleigh rides in winter, buggy rides in summer — and singing school. It is on the way home from singing school one day that Laura and Almanzo become engaged. Then they are married and Laura goes to live with him in another little house on a claim. Ages 10 and up. Cloth (6¾ x 9¾). $2.00.

Published by
HARPER & BROTHERS
Established 1817

This publicity flyer about Laura and the Little House books was sent to readers in the 1940's by Laura's publishers, Harper & Brothers.

eyes; I have seen them purple. Baby-fine, pure white hair. She wears it cut short and permanent-waved. She's very dainty and well-groomed, and speaks and moves quickly,

sometimes vivaciously. But her character is Scotch; she holds a purpose or an opinion like granite. She's not at all "Sot in her *ways*" but she is in every other way.

She wrote the "Little House" series first as an autobiography,* in a rather matter-of-fact style. I believe she relied on the facts themselves for interest and drama. Editors and publishers refused the book. Then she determined to save at least the stories her father had told her when she was a child. She was deeply devoted to her father and to his memory, as seen from her books. So she wrote *Little House in the Big Woods*. It was re-written perhaps a dozen times.

All her writing before that had been matter-of-fact in style; she had done some articles for national magazines and was on the staff of the Capper Publications who published the *Missouri Ruralist*. She was Poultry Editor for a farm paper; it is characteristic that she began a series of short pieces on breeds of poultry, without realizing how many there were. The series went on and on, and on. The editors tried to get her to stop it; she would not, saying that once begun, it must be finished.

I was living on the farm at the time she wrote *Little House in the Big Woods*, and read the manuscripts. I'd cross out great chunks, telling her the style was dull, that she needed more vividness, more color and contrast. So she would do it all over again. She writes in longhand, with pencil, in big, rough paper 5 cent school tablets. That's the Scotch, plus the hun-

---

*Laura entitled this unpublished manuscript *Pioneer Girl.*

gry pioneer; she doesn't waste an inch of cheapest paper. She fills six or seven of these tablets. Then she does over the job, writing in bits in more tablets, cutting out these bits and attaching them with pins to the original copy. She draws maps of the places she is writing about, and follows her characters over them, to get the scenic descriptions accurately checked with her memories. It is amazing to me that she developed the style of writing that she did; there were only streaks of it in her first attempts. A sentence would jump right up at you from a dead level, as if it had been done by another person. There is hardly a trace of her writing style in her letters even yet.

Since I have not been on the farm since she wrote her earliest books, she has always sent me the big bundles of the bulky tablets to criticize. But she has earned her own place as a writer; she would have done it with no advice from anybody. She and her work should be considered entirely independently. She is an extreme individualist (so am I), and she resents being described as inept reports used sometimes to describe her, as the "Mother of Rose Wilder Lane." I think myself that such a phrase is just cause for resentment.

She writes a verse in each of her books that she sends me. The last one, in *These Happy Golden Years* ends the series with

And so farewell to childhood days,
Their joys and hopes and fears,
But Father's voice and his fiddle's song
Go echoing down the years.

I think her deepest feeling about the whole work she has done is that now her father will not be forgotten. She is giving his fiddle, with a set of her books, to the South Dakota State Historical Museum.

Her last book tells of her marriage, which was not long before the beginning of the seven years' drought in the Dust Bowl which coincided with a world-wide financial collapse to make, eventually, the "Panic" of 1893, or as it's called now, the "Depression." In 1894, with $100 my mother accumulated sewing in a dressmaker's shop, we left Dakota in a covered wagon for Missouri. The $100 bought 40 acres of sub-marginal hill land, about eight inches of clay sub-soil grown up in scrub timber, with a one-room cabin on it. There was a $300 mortgage on the land, at the rate then usual, 12%. My mother hates debt.

Today, the farmhouse stands on top of a gently sloping knoll of about three acres, with centuries-old oaks on it; the slope in spring is so covered with hen's foot violets that at a distance, it looks blue. My mother prefers wild flowers to cultivated ones and Missouri is always a mass of wild flowers; the knoll changes color all summer.

The farmhouse kitchen is the first of the family triumphs, the one-room frame house into which we moved after some time in the log cabin. It is completely modern now, with electric range, refrigerator and cabinets. Attached is the dining room, a large screened dining and sitting porch; a large south bedroom with bath, my mother's little office where she wrote the "Little House" series, and the large living room. The living room is entirely paneled in oak, cut from the farm, milled and waxed; it has a small oak-paneled library or large book-nook, separated by a half-partition, and a large fireplace and large windows. Upstairs there are three bedrooms, one a sleeping porch.

There's a narrow back stairs, ingeniously going down between the kitchen and dining room with cupboards built in under it. On the stair my mother was once climbing with a five-gallon crockery jar of boiling water, to keep warm some baby chicks she was temporarily sheltering in the attic because of unseasonable storms. The bottom fell out of the jar, and believe it or not, my mother went down the stair faster than the water did, and escaped scalding. She's still quicker than a flash and stronger than a little French horse.

My mother is a very good cook, though she doesn't like cooking, and a good housekeeper, though she doesn't like housework either. She is handicapped because her hands are so small; I don't mean deformed at all, but it takes larger hands with bigger grip to do housework easily. She does no gardening. She doesn't like, indeed she suffered, from the dust on her hands; I believe she mentioned this in her books when she picked up potatoes and pulled turnips.

My father is nearly ninety; he hasn't gray hair yet and uses glasses only to read fine print. He can no longer get automobile insurance because of his age, but he drives the Chrysler car anyway. Just before the war he drove my mother to De Smet and the Black Hills. She always sits beside him and "backseat drives" so that he can enjoy the landscape without any worry.

The Wilders have been farmers since King John's time in England and since 1632 in this country. I mentioned this once in *Saturday Evening Post*, and a howl came in from a Wilder who wanted it corrected, saying that the Wilders were English gentry. I replied that I speak American; the English word is "gentry"; the American word is "farmer." "Farmer" in English means "share-cropper" in American. The English Wilders are still gentry, but the American Wilders are farmers. The protester was Librarian of Dartmouth College.

Like most sensible farmers, my father was doing contour plowing, stopping erosion and practicing soil conservation when he was a boy in northern New York state, and has done so ever since. My parents know every bird that comes to their farm. They feed the quail through hard winters. During ice storms, my father walks over the whole place, putting out grain for the wild birds. They permit no hunting, even of rabbits.

My mother is an extreme individualist (so am I). These United States are a very interesting place; my mother thinks so. I know she hopes her books will give that general impression to the coming generations of Americans.

Soon after Little House in the Big Woods *was published, Laura Ingalls Wilder started receiving admiring mail from her readers. Her stories rang so true, and her characters were so tenderly*

Laura at age seventy. This photograph was one of three taken in September 1937 to promote Laura's appearance at a book fair in Detroit.

drawn, that those who read about the Ingalls and Wilder families longed to know what happened to the people in Laura's books. For over twenty years Laura personally answered her ever-increasing

mail load, and her publishers assisted by distributing a printed let-
ter she had composed to readers. During the summer of 1943,
despite being "very busy canning berries and garden stuff," she
composed a letter telling about her family and describing her pre-
sent life with Almanzo.

At the age of seventy-six, Laura decided to write no more. She
had an open invitation from her publishers to write more books,
but she declined, choosing instead to devote her time to her hus-
band, who was eighty-six. "There are of course a number of books
that might be written," she admitted, "of our ups and downs, of
sickness and loss, of gains and success, for as with everyone our life
has been full of such things." Fortunately for her interested readers,
though, Laura shared more information about herself and her life
in the Ozarks in the following autobiographical account. These
writings offer a glimpse into how Laura saw her later years.

My Family

It is a long story, filled with sunshine and shadow, that we
have lived since the "Little House" books. After our marriage
Almanzo and I lived on our homestead claim near De Smet.
During this time, our daughter Rose was born. She was born
in December, but named for the wild prairie roses of the
summer before.

We were enticed from the prairie land of long, cold winters to the "Land of the Big Red Apple," as the Ozarks of
Missouri were advertised then. Peaches were said to grow
wild in the corners of rail fences, the only kind of fences
there were. We came to the Ozarks, Almanzo, Rose and I, in

a covered wagon in 1894. There we pioneered again, this time in hilly, timbered country.

We bought a rough, rocky forty acres of land, with five acres cleared of timber and a one-room log house, where the only way for light to enter with the door shut was through cracks between logs where the chinking had fallen out. Another little house!

Through the years we added to our land until we owned 185 acres, cleared except for wood lots left to furnish wood to burn and fence posts. We built the ten room Rocky Ridge Farmhouse of materials from the farm itself, except for the pine siding on the outside. The oak frame of the house, oak paneling, solid oak beams and stairs in the living room are from our own timber, hand finished and an enormous fireplace is made of three large rocks dug from our own ground. The chimney is built of our own rocks.

With our own hands and strength we cleared the land and planted crops among the rocks. I pulled one end of a crosscut saw to help Almanzo cut down standing trees, helped saw them up into rail lengths and while he split the lengths into rails, I piled brush for bonfires.

Rose played along the creek, helped pick berries, peaches and apples, and after frost in the fall when leaves of forest trees were aflame with color, we gathered walnuts, hickory nuts and hazelnuts and stored them for winter as the busy squirrels were doing. During school terms Rose walked or rode her donkey the mile to school in town.

For recreation we rode horseback down the woods trails

or took buggy rides on the out roads, on the best of which we needed to be careful not to drive against the stumps of trees left in the road. We tamed the wild birds and squirrels as they were always around the house. We had our cottage organ and always our books and papers, chief among them still *The Youth's Companion* and Mother's church paper, *The Advance*. I like to crochet and knit and embroider, to piece quilts and quilt them. I have done and still do a great deal of such work.

You may be interested to know what happened to some of the other people you met in my books. . . .

After I married, Pa and Ma lived on their homestead until it was sold and they moved to De Smet. Pa did carpenter work in town, which was still growing. He never got over his longing to go further west, but realized it was better for the family to stay where they already had a home. Pa built a house in the residential part of town, near church and neighbors.

Mary graduated from the Iowa College for the Blind in 1889. Her part in an entertainment given by her literary society was an essay entitled, "Memory." You may remember in the books I told of Mary's remarkable memory. In the graduating exercises on June 10, Mary read another essay, "Bide a Wee and Dinna Weary," which showed the influence of Pa's old Scot songs.

After her graduation, Mary lived happily at home with her music, and her raised print and Braille books. She knitted and sewed and took part in the housework.

After Carrie finished high school she went into the office

of the town newspaper, *The De Smet News*, where, as was customary in small towns of that day, she set type, read proof, wrote the items of town news and was a general helper of Carter P. Sherwood, editor and publisher.

Grace graduated from high school and later married and went to live on her husband's farm near Manchester, the little town where Laura spent a summer with Mrs. McKee.* This left only Ma and Pa and Mary and Carrie at home.

Carrie was never strong and because of poor health was ordered by her doctor to the Black Hills to stay. There she married a mine owner near Mount Rushmore and is living in her home there now. Carrie is a widow now and she and I are the only ones of our family still living.

Uncle Tom went West again, taking his family with him, to the state of Washington, where he engaged in the lumbering business and after a few years was killed in an accident at a flume. His children and their families were still in Washington the last I knew.

Yesterday I received a letter from Cousin Lena's daughter saying she died in June. You met her in *By the Shores of Silver Lake*, riding and driving the black ponies. Cousins Alice and Ella, with their families, went to California about the time we left De Smet. They are all gone but their children are still in California. Cousin Peter went to Florida, married, and died there.

You see the characters in my books have been scattered

---

* Described in *These Happy Golden Years*.

far and near since I told of them in my stories of so long ago and far away.

Almanzo is 86 years old and I am 76. We still call our place Rocky Ridge Farm, but we are not really farming now. We were proud of our dairy and poultry farm, our Jersey cows and Leghorn hens. But is has been increasingly difficult to get help and lately impossible to do so at wages the farm could pay, so we have sold the land with another house on the east end of the farm and another small house and land to the north. Now we have only 130 acres of land. Our land is now all in pasture and meadow, which we rent, and a large timber lot.

Mr. Wilder cares for our four milk goats and two calves in the morning, while I prepare our seven o'clock breakfast. Then he works in the garden or the shop where he loves to tinker while I do up the housework and go down the hill to the mail box for the mail. I take our big brown-and-white spotted bulldog with me and we go for a half mile walk before we come back.

After that the day is always full, for I do all my own work, and to care for a ten room house is no small job. Besides the cooking and baking there is churning to do. I make all our own butter from cream off the goat milk.

There is always sewing on hand and my mending is seldom finished. The town is near and I must go to church, aid society, socials, be entertained and entertain my friends now and then.

When Almanzo and the car go anywhere I always go

along, for I love to go for a drive as well as I ever did. We don't drive horses now. We drive a Chrysler.

And when the day is over and evening comes we read our papers and magazines or play a game of cribbage. If we want music we turn on the radio.

It has been a good and pleasant life, filled with work and play, careful planning and saving. What we accomplished was without help of any kind from anyone.

OF TIME, LIFE, AND ETERNITY

Laura Ingalls Wilder held private her most personal beliefs and thoughts, so it seems almost invasive to speculate upon her religion. She transcends any effort by any sect or creed to claim a shared faith or denomination; her values and morals stood for more universal qualities of courage, honesty, kindness, and compassion, as her public and private writings indicate. Like those of other uncommon characters in history, Laura's appeal and influence are widespread; her philosophy is best understood through the principles she practiced and the life she lived.

Although formal religious training was sporadic for Laura Ingalls while she grew up in a pioneer family, what she missed in church and Sunday school was more than compensated for through the teachings of her parents. Reading from the Bible, memorizing and quoting its verses, and singing the hymns of the era along with Pa's fiddle were routine activities in the Ingalls home.

Although church life was often mentioned in the Little House books, only once did Laura write of personal revelation during her childhood. As a twelve-year-old, she was asked to serve as a companion to a family friend, Sadie Hurley, on an isolated homestead near Walnut Grove, Minnesota. As she recalled the incident:

Ma did not like to take me out of school, but finally consented, and taking my school books I went . . . driving through the cold and snow to a little claim shanty two miles in the country. My bed was curtained off from the rest of the room with a calico curtain.

I stayed with Sadie two weeks while John made up his crop of broom straw into brooms to be sold in town. The days were lonely and I was homesick. I knew things were not going well at home because Pa could not get much work and we were in need of money to live on. One night while saying my prayers before going to bed, this feeling of homesickness and worry was worse than usual but gradually I had a sense of a hovering, encompassing Presence, a Power comforting and sustaining and I thought in surprise, "This is what men call God."

The tenets of faith that Laura learned at home and in the Congregational and Methodist churches and Sunday schools of Walnut Grove, Burr Oak, and De Smet supplied her with a firm foundation of plain Protestant theology. As a teenager in De Smet, she occasionally wrote poetry that incorporated some of these tenets.

Love Your Enemies
Love your enemies.
Oh my God! how hard is that command
To keep.
To love one's enemies, love must be
As broad as the ocean,
And as deep.
We can not do it,
Oh my God! unless thou help us

In thy love.
Oh give us strength to do thy will
Great God of earth
And heaven above

Another poem of praise shows the influence of the frequent hymn singing within Laura's family; they sang hymns from the Pure Gold Songbook *and* The Psalter.

Praise Ye the Lord
Praise ye the Lord
For His goodness and mercy!
Goodness and mercy unto us He has shown.
His loving eye watches in tenderness over us,
However far from His path we may roam.
Praise ye the Lord!

Praise ye the Lord
That unto the weak He gives strength!
Strength when sorely oppressed by the strong.
The oppressed always conquer, for He always aids them,
'Though their heart may be faint, and the struggle seem
    long.
Praise ye the Lord!

Praise ye the Lord
That He cares for our troubles!

Troubles that to Him must seem very small.
That He sees, understands them, and pitieth His
   children,
Like as a Father, who comes at their call,
Praise ye the Lord!

Praise ye the Lord.
That He pardons and forgives us!
Pardons all who repent and turn from the wrong!
Oh! Praise ye the Lord, for His goodness and mercy
Praise him in heart and praise Him in song.
Praise ye the Lord!

Such hardships as poverty, ill health, the loss of a child, and separation from those she loved would test Laura througout her lifetime. But like her father, Laura thought optimistically and always looked ahead to better times. As she approached middle age, she became increasingly thoughtful about the life she had lived. Driving west with Rose in their Buick in 1925, Laura saw the Rocky Mountains before her, and the sight made her reflect on what she wanted her role in the world to be. She mused:

The way before us rose; almost imperceptibly higher and ever higher. It was all so familiar that it seemed to me that I must find my lost youth just over the horizon and the dreams of life's springtime waiting once again to be realized. All day I followed the road of memories into that land

Laura, Rose, and Isabelle, the family Buick, in the Tennessee Pass, Colorado, en route to California.

of Dreams until I felt once more that the only thing in life really worthwhile was their fulfillment.

To be broad in outlook as the plains themselves; free as the cloud shadows that drift over, and brave as the small creatures that make their homes upon them; to be clean and pure like the air and strong like the winds that sweep over the uplands.

What greater thing could be won from life than the dreams of youth come true?

Laura and Almanzo at home during the summer of 1942; she was seventy-five, he was eighty-five.

Laura knew from life's hard experience that dreams were sometimes stalled, and hardships could arrive in plenty. But many years of perspective showed her that no difficulty is permanent, and that one of life's certainties was that "this too shall pass away."

This poem reveals that Laura would sometimes apply a stoic rationale to the adventure of life.

Have you what your heart desires:
Are you happy and glad and gay?
Does the sun shine bright,
And the world move right:
Is Fortune smiling to-day?
Fortune's a fickle jade
And she never comes to stay.
So don't expect she'll tarry long
But enjoy her while you may.
Then bask in the sunshine now.
Be gay while the gods allow.
Drink your cup of bliss
While it's yet to-day
Ere "This too shall pass away."

Is the sun behind the clouds
And your plans all gone askew?
While your fortune halts,
Are your friends all false,
And your enemies "besting" you?
The storm will not last long

Laura is wearing one of her favorite velvet dresses in this picture, taken in the spring of 1954.

The fiercer, the sooner done.
True friends will come as false ones go
The shadows pass from the sun.
Then just keep working along,
Through bad, or worse, or wrong,
Let the storm clouds lower,
And the storm winds play,
For "This too shall pass away."

This world is a stage all set,
And we are the actors there,
With the lights all lit
And the music all fit
And the critics everywhere.
Some act the hero's part
And some are villains gay,
Some come on with a song and dance
That drives dull care away.
Then do your part with a song.
Your "turn" will not be long
And you'll win applause,
While you make your play:
Then "This too shall pass away."

Despite her national renown as an author and the knowledge that her books would be read by future generations of children, Laura was always modest when she considered her fame. She never thought of her many awards and significant honors

In facing a crisis read 46 Psalm
When discouraged   "   23+24 "
Lonely or fearful   "   27 "
Planning budget   " St. Luke chapter 19
To live successfuly with others read
Romans, chapter 12
Sick or in pain read 91 Psalm
When you travel carry with you 121 Psalm
When very weary read Mathew 11 – 28 & 30
and Romans 8 – 31 to 39
When things are going from bad to worse
2 Timothy – 3d.
When friends go back on you hold to
1 Corinthians 13th.
For inward peace the 14th. chapter of St John, Gos
To avoid misfortune Mathew 7 – 24 to 27
For record of what trust in God can do Hebrews – 11
If you are having to put up a fight – the
end of Ephesions
When you have sinned read 1 John 3 – 1 to 21
And make Psalm 51 your prayer

Laura's favorite Bible verses.

as personal achievements. As she clearly stated in this poem, her
role was to preserve the courage and accomplishments of all the
pioneers she wrote about.

Some day when I am dead and gone
The flowers will blossom just the same,
Some day my face will be forgot,
My only memory be a name,
And then my name will fade away
Clean blotted from the page of time,
And with them both will surely go
All knowledge of this bit of rhyme.
But still I hope in that far day,
True hearts will prove themselves akin,
To the brave hearts of those old days
My memory has wandered in:
That when their time of trial comes,
'Twill strengthen faith and banish fears,
Whene'er they chance to think upon
The history of the pioneers.
With courage high they journeyed far;
With faith they traveled day by day;
And ever leading on ahead
The star of hope shone on their way.

*Through more than sixty years in Mansfield, Laura was associated
with the town's Methodist church, though interestingly, neither she
nor Almanzo ever joined officially. They attended Sunday services,
entertained the minister, and were involved in the congregation's
efforts to build a church. At home the Bible was a frequently con-
sulted resource. The big black embossed family Bible, a gift to the
Wilders from Pa and Ma soon after their wedding, was always a*

visible part of the household, but Laura preferred her own small well-thumbed Sunday school Bible. Surprising as it may seem for one who was a bookworm, and who accumulated a whole library of volumes, Laura evidently considered the Bible her only needed religious text. Only one other book in her collection is of a religious type: Glenn Clark's The Soul's Secret Desire. *From this book she copied a line she thought significant: "Prayer is the Soul's sincere desire, uttered or unexpressed." In her later years, her Bible was a fixture on the table next to her favorite rocking chair, as familiar to visitors as the piles of mail that always accumulated in the same place. In ink, on the same soft lined tablet paper she used to write her Little House books, Laura wrote down a guide for important Bible references.*

It seems appropriate to end this collection with a poem Laura wrote about eternity. She did not write much about death; perhaps her stoic approach to life allowed her to view death as an inevitable part of human existence. This poem expresses Laura's vision that beyond life and beyond death, there is eternity.

Facing the illimitable ocean
There are no bounds,
Earth blends with sky
And reaches on into infinitude.
Even so my life facing the future
Sees no end.
But finite blends with infinite
And reaches on into the far beyond.